The Far D

The People and History of Haast and Jackson Bay

Julia Bradshaw

Otago University Press

Dedicated to Ruby, Allan, Henry, Des, Ann, Bernie, Myra, Betty, and Mary

Published by Otago University Press
Level 1, 398 Cumberland Street,
PO Box 56, Dunedin, New Zealand
Fax: 64 3 479 8385
Email: university.press@otago.ac.nz
Web : www.otago.ac.nz/press

First published 2001, reprinted 2010
Copyright © Julia Bradshaw 2001
ISBN 978-1-877276-07-1

Cover design by Anneloes Douglas
Printed through Condor Production Ltd, Hong Kong

Contents

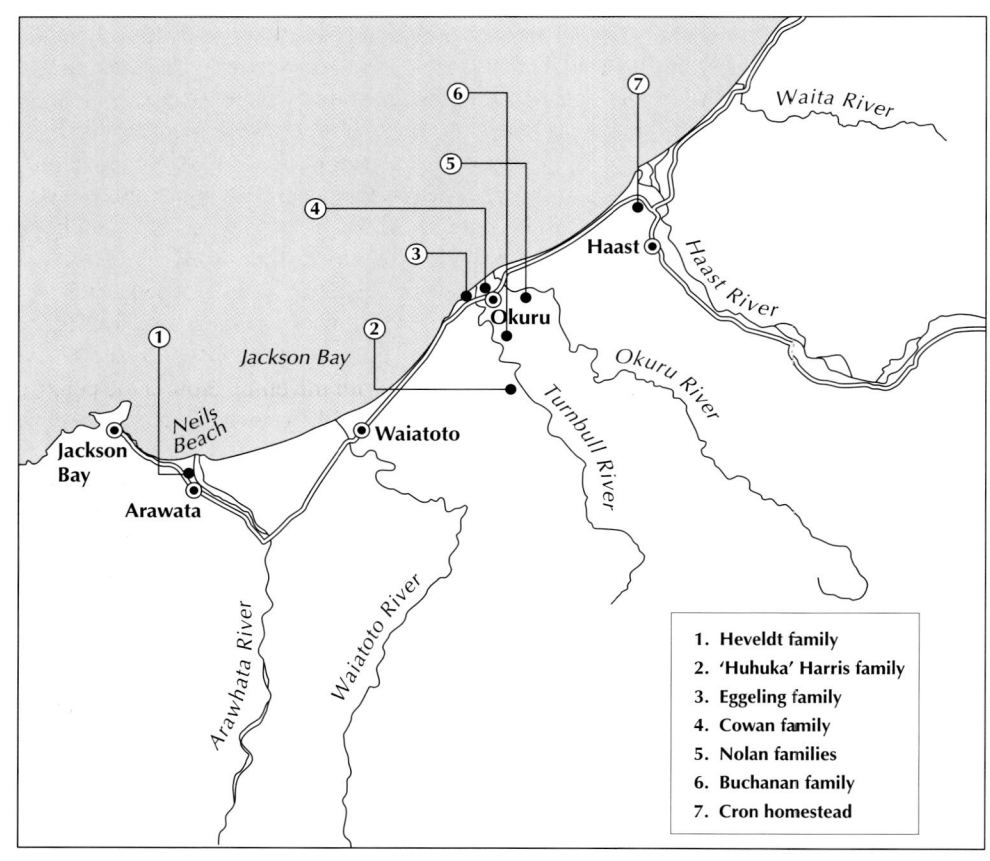

Family homes of the people interviewed in this book.

Acknowledgements

This book would not have been possible without the generosity of the people whose recorded interviews contribute so much to it. Ruby, Allan, Henry, Des, Ann, Bernie, Myra, Betty and Mary freely gave their time and shared with me their memories of growing up and living in South Westland. As well, they were generous with the loan of photographs, as were their family and friends, who also provided additional information.

The Haast Oral History Project, upon which this book is based, was made possible by a grant from the Australian Sesquicentennial Gift Trust for Awards in Oral History, Historical Branch, Department of Internal Affairs (now the History Group, Ministry for Culture and Heritage). Of the nine interviewees, only three still lived in the Haast district. The grant assisted with the costs associated with travelling around the country to conduct the interviews. I am very grateful for the financial assistance that made both the project and this book possible.

I would also like to thank the following people, who helped with information and photos: Rosalie Buchanan, Ted Buchanan, John and Kay Cowan, Maryann Cowan, Eunice Cron, Cliff Cron and his daughter Diane Houston, Myra Fulton, Francis and Reta Heveldt, Brian Jones, Paul Beauchamp Legg, Bill Nolan, Neville Peat, Mary Savage and Richard Waugh. Every effort has been made to gain permission for use of photographs but it wasn't always possible to trace the owner of the copyright.

Thanks are also due to Peter Read and Mary Rooney of the West Coast Historical Museum, the late David McDonald and staff at the Hocken Library, Dunedin, and the helpful staff at Archives New Zealand in Christchurch and at the Alexander Turnbull Library in Wellington.

And last, but most of all, I would like to thank my partner, Eddie Newman, for his never-ending support and encouragement during the course of this long project.

'There is so much rain here. You're in a sou'wester riding coat three-quarters of your life, anyhow. Old Paddy Nolan, he was the only one I knew that was never ever worried about it. He'd ride through a river and he'd just drag his feet through. He wouldn't even bother lifting them up to stop them from getting wet. He used to say, 'It won't go past your skin boy.' Henry Buchanan, 1996

Introduction

The Haast district was (and some might say still is) a frontier community. Until the late 1950s there were only bush tracks connecting Haast with Hokitika (180 miles away) and Wanaka (ninety miles). For supplies settlers relied on a coastal shipping service which called every two to three months. Horse and human muscle were used for carrying in small goods, and for carrying out anyone needing emergency medical care. In 1960 a road was built over Haast Pass, linking Haast to Wanaka. The Haast district was finally connected to the rest of the West Coast in 1965, when the road between the Franz Josef and Fox glaciers and Haast was completed.

This book is based on a series of oral history interviews I conducted with people who grew up in the Haast district during the 1920s and 1930s. These men and women knew a way of life which had virtually disappeared a generation earlier in the rest of New Zealand. Here, for example, were people who could remember when a serious illness meant being carried on a stretcher for several days to get to the nearest road. And it wasn't just roads that were slow to reach the Haast district. Radio and television were late arrivals, too. Evenings were spent telling stories, and the people of Haast were (and some still are) wonderful storytellers.

As the interviews progressed, it soon became apparent that these people had a wonderful talent for mimicry. When an interviewee told me what someone else had said, he or she would invariably (and unselfconsciously) mimic the original speaker. Unfortunately it is impossible to reproduce this quality in a written work. I have, however, tried to keep each person's manner of speaking alive in 'their' chapter of the book. The interviewees are memorable and special people: this, together with their isolated and innovative lifestyles, gives their stories a distinctive flavour.

The first three chapters are intended to give the reader a brief background to the area, with an overview of the first and later settlers and also of the Special Settlement Scheme at Jackson Bay in 1875. Most of the interviewees are descended from some of those resilient pioneers. A lucky find at Sound Archives/Nga Taonga Korero (Christchurch) meant that I was able to give readers a first-hand account of settlement in the late 1870s and 1880s.

The remaining chapters consist of the interviewees'

accounts of life in the Haast district. These are edited transcripts of the oral history interviews; as such, they reflect the interviewees' own take on the history of the area. These chapters are arranged according to age. Ruby Hill (née Eggeling) is first, having been born in 1907, and Mary Jones (née Cowell), the youngest interviewee, born in 1928, has the final place in the book. As the interviewees invariably used imperial measurements, these have been used throughout the book.

The title, *The Far Downers*, comes from the name given to the occupants of the far south by residents of the more northern settlements, such as Whataroa, Weheka (Fox Glacier) and Bruce Bay. The people of the Haast district lived 'Far Down' the coast, beyond the reach of road and adequate communication, effectively cut off by one hundred miles of rugged terrain. It was by no means a derogatory statement, it was simply a statement of fact: these people lived as far down on the West Coast as it was possible to live, barring the attempted settlement of Martins Bay (in 1870) and the occasional settler in Fiordland.

I hope that readers will enjoy meeting the Far Downers as I much as I have.

JULIA BRADSHAW
Hokitika, 2001

A Note

Arawata/Arawhata: Maori knew the river as Arawhata but when it was mapped by Europeans (c. 1860s) it became Arawata. In 1990 the New Zealand Geographic Board changed the name back to Arawhata, but in referring to the township (at Jackson Bay) and area of rural sections (beside the Arawhata River) established in 1875, I have used the spelling of that time, i.e. Arawata township and Arawata settlement, respectively.

Ted Cron on the old Maori trail to the West Coast via Tioripatea, Haast Pass.
Courtesy of Cliff Cron

Wooden canoe prow in the shape of a dog's head, found at Jackson Bay. Department of Conservation, Hokitika

The modern fishing fleet at Jackson Bay. Julia Bradshaw

Chapter 1

Early Settlers and Visitors

The first settlers: Maori in the Haast district

About thirty miles south of Haast, Jackson Bay is the only natural harbour on the wave-lashed West Coast of the South Island. Today it is home to most of South Westland's fishing fleet, but in past times it was important to another group of fishing people, the Maori.

Maori probably arrived on the coast in about A.D. 900, with the tribal make-up of the area changing several times over the next 1000 years. There was a string of settlement along the West Coast, with villages in South Westland being at Okahu (near Arawhata River) and at Whakatipu wai-tai (Martins Bay), and the main settlement at Mahitahi (Bruce Bay). In the Haast district, sites of occupation have been found near the Haast River, at Okuru and in the Jackson Bay area. Camping sites have been found elsewhere along the coast.

Artefacts have been found in numerous places, especially in the vicinity of Jackson Bay, suggesting that this was an important place many years ago. Items found include nephrite adzes, gouges, lure shanks, sandstone files, pendants and fishing sinkers. The village of Okahu (named after Kahu, a chief slain there), with its favourable location at the mouth of the Arawhata River only a few miles from Jackson Bay, was probably the main settlement in the Haast district. From Okahu there was access to pounamu (New Zealand jade), which could be found south of Jackson Bay. Archaeological evidence shows that pounamu was being worked locally by A.D. 1200 and that this highly prized and durable stone was widely traded throughout Aotearoa/New Zealand.

The forests and lagoons of South Westland provided abundant food. Eels and ducks were plentiful in the wetland areas and kereru (pigeons), kakapo, kiwi and kaka were easily caught in the forest. In the spring, rivers teemed with whitebait, which were caught in fine nets and dried in the sun for later consumption. At Jackson Bay, there was easy access to seals, crayfish, and shellfish such as paua and mussels. The natural harbour would have been an ideal spot to launch canoes for offshore fishing of species such as terakihi and cod.

The relatively peaceful life of South Westland Maori was disturbed in about 1805 by the appearance of the Otago chief Te Matehaere, who led a large war party of two hundred or more men through the Hollyford Valley and then north from Martins Bay to Nelson, killing

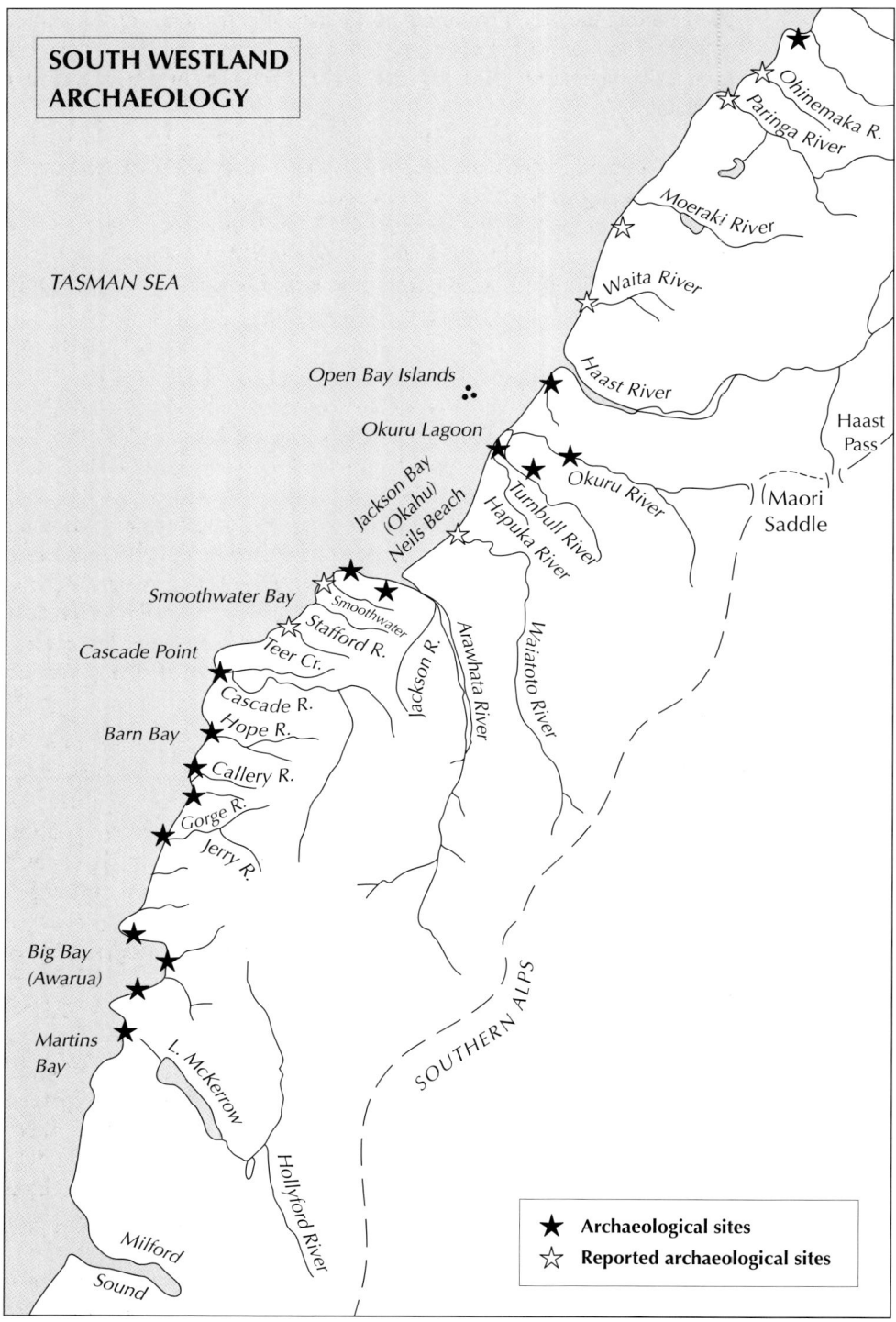

SOUTH WESTLAND ARCHAEOLOGY

TASMAN SEA

Ohinemaka R.

Paringa River

Moeraki River

Waita River

Haast River

Haast Pass

Maori Saddle

Open Bay Islands

Okuru Lagoon

Okuru River

Jackson Bay (Okahu)

Turnbull River

Neils Beach

Hapuka River

Waiatoto River

Arawhata River

Jackson R.

Smoothwater Bay

Smoothwater

Stafford R.

Cascade Point

Teer Cr.

Cascade R.

Barn Bay

Hope R.

Callery R.

Gorge R.

Jerry R.

Big Bay (Awarua)

Martins Bay

L. McKerrow

SOUTHERN ALPS

Hollyford River

Milford Sound

★ Archaeological sites
☆ Reported archaeological sites

people along the way. Five or ten years later, Wharekai, a Kai Tahu chief who lived in North Canterbury, led a force into Westland. They travelled over Rakamaunikura (Harper Pass) and took control of much of South Westland.[1]

In 1826 the sealer John Boultbee reported a village of three hundred people near Jackson Bay, presumably the Okahu settlement. While camping north of Haast, Boultbee and his party were attacked by a party of Maori, possibly in revenge for an attack by other sealers. Two of the sealers were killed in the skirmish before the Maori retreated, some of them injured. Boultbee and his companions hastily withdrew to Open Bay Islands and then travelled south to join their ship.

Other sealing gangs, hearing of the attack on Boultbee, were quick to retaliate. One band headed by the notorious Thomas Chaseland attacked Okahu, first shooting from their boats and, on landing, killing anyone who had not managed to escape into the bush. An elderly Maori from Southland gave the following account to Herries Beattie in about 1918:

When Chaseland was roused he became a frenzied fiend. Among his other acts he seized a child, Ramirikiri, whose father and mother had been killed, and dashed her head on a rock and left her for dead. After the sealers had done all the mischief they could they left and the surviving natives crept out of the bush and returned to their desolate homes. They found the little girl living and revived her and she died at Colac, an old woman, some fifteen or sixteen years ago.[2]

Incidents such as these, and the introduction of smallpox and other diseases, would have dramatically reduced the size of the Okahu settlement. A census taken in 1852 listed the population as fourteen, with Chief Wharekai being the head man. Also living at Okahu was Te Kanau, a tohunga who could reputedly make a woman follow him against her will. Wharekai's wife, Kupenu, was also regarded as a tohunga.[3] While settlements at Whakatipu wai-tai and Mahitahi were dominated by a different hapu (sub-tribe), there seems to have been much trade and travel between these places and Okahu. Indeed, Chief Tutoko, his family and others (numbering seventeen) had shifted only recently from Okahu to Martins Bay at the time of the 1852 census.[4]

Maori living at Okahu frequently helped European travellers. John Lort Stokes, travelling around the southwest coast of the South Island on the *Acheron* in 1850, traded for potatoes grown at the village. In 1857, eight crew members from the barque *Pacific*, who had either deserted or been wrecked, were given food and directions before travelling north to Nelson. They left a boy of sixteen, William Miller, who was too weak to walk, with the 'native sealers' at Jackson Bay.[5]

In August 1862, Charles Ollivier explored the Jackson Bay area with his brother Claude, and met 'four natives, one old

Map of known Maori occupation sites in the Haast district. Many more sites have been reported, but not verified.

After Hooker, 1986

man and three women', other Maori having gone to the Otago goldfields. Presumably the old man was Wharekai, although it might also have been Tutoko with his wife and daughters, as this family appears to have travelled up and down the coast. Communication was difficult, but the Olliviers were shown a document from the government granting the Maori land and later, when the Olliviers were short of food, they were offered some of the Maoris' meagre supply of potatoes.[6]

In about August 1866 Chief Wharekai died at Okahu. Three Maori women were still living there at that time but there are no further references to them. It is probable that they shifted north to be with relatives living at Okarito. From the mid-1860s onwards, Maori in South Westland were based in the Bruce Bay district.[7]

European visitors to the Haast district

Open Bay was the name Captain Cook gave to the bight between Cascade Point and Arnott Point, when he sailed up the coast in 1770. The name stuck to the islands in the bight, but other features gained individual European names as time went on. The name Jackson Bay first appeared on a map in 1844 and was so named by sealers, possibly after William Jackson, a member of a sealing gang marooned on Open Bay Islands for over three years.[8]

The value of Jackson Bay as a harbour was noted by early seafarers. Sealers and whalers called into the bay to obtain wood and water, and also used it as a more permanent base. The *New Zealand Book of Shipwrecks, 1795-1970* records that in January 1849 the schooner *Kate* was wrecked at Jackson Bay, while endeavouring to collect oil from Captain Salmon's whaling station. Later arrivals referred to debris left by whalers and to areas where trees had been felled.[9]

Claude and Charles Ollivier were just two of a number of Europeans who visited Jackson Bay looking for new country or treasure of some sort. They left Canterbury in August 1862 in the schooner *Ada* and sailed down the West Coast, looking for land suitable for sheep farming. Cascade Point seemed promising and the Olliviers decided to investigate. Soon after their arrival at Jackson Bay, a northerly storm blew up and the schooner had to take to the open sea, leaving the brothers with a tent and a supply of food.

Several rough days were spent travelling towards Cascade Point before the pair turned back, 'wretched, torn and bleeding'. They sat dismally in their tent and waited for the return of the *Ada*. Claude was suffering from bad headaches and remained in the tent, while Charles searched for firewood and birds to eat. Their small supply of food was supplemented only by the occasional pigeon, and the gift of potatoes by local Maori. Finally, the *Ada* reappeared in the bay. The brothers were

Entries from the diary kept by Charles Ollivier while at Jackson Bay

August 18 – Last night a dog got into our tent, evidently the same that stole our cheese the previous night, so we shot him.

August 20 – Our neighbour the old Maori brought us to day a small basket of potatoes about the size of marbles, but they were, I believe, the best he had. He asked us if we had seen his dog, but having just then caught sight of the dead dog he got into a violent passion, but it was thrown away on us, as we did not know what he was saying. A few sticks of tobacco however soon restored peace.[10]

The grave of Claude Ollivier at Jackson Bay. Charles Ollivier describes his brother's burial in August 1862: 'We made the best coffin that circumstances admitted of, and at two p.m. we all went on shore on our mournful errand: We selected a spot for the grave where we found the ruins of some old sealing station, and the Captain having read the burial service, we laid with aching hearts, on that dreary inhospitable shore, all that was left of him who was the loved of all.'[11]
Photo by Julia Bradshaw

immediately taken on board, but Claude's health did not improve and he died in his sleep on 27 August 1862, aged twenty-two. His death is a poignant reminder of the high price paid by colonists in their search for a new life.[12]

In 1863 a party of goldminers from the *Nugget* spent several months prospecting in the Jackson Bay district. Local Maori told them that at one time there had often been ten vessels in the bay. The miners themselves encountered several whaling vessels. In June 1863 Captain Pennyman brought a barque into the bay to collect wood and water. He reported that he had 180 tons of sperm oil on board and had been whaling on the coast for twenty-five years. Captain McGrath, in the whaling brig *Grecian* (209 tons with fourteen crew), also called at the bay.[13]

In early 1863, Europeans began using the old Maori trail from Otago to the West Coast via Haast Pass. Otago Maori named the pass Tioripatea, as the leader of parties travelling along this route would call 'tiori patea' (the way ahead is clear) when the summit was reached.

Charles Cameron reached the pass in January 1863 and was followed by Julius von Haast and party, who spent thirty days travelling through to the Tasman Sea, arriving at Haast Beach on 20 February 1863. Haast publicised the route and it was used occasionally by hardy

Through Haast Pass in 1865	We turned in, and slept soundly until suddenly awakened by a most unearthly roar, resembling that of a donkey in distress. Doherty [sic] sprang up and seized the tomahawk, while I collared the gun, and we rushed out of the tent in pitch darkness. Spriggins [the dog] kept silent, but alert, and at the next roar he made a spring and seized the disturber, a large fat kakapo. Though we had seen a stuffed one, neither of us had ever met one in its native haunts, and we had no idea that a bird could possibly utter such an appalling, nerve-splitting yell. Of course, we cooked that fellow for our breakfast, and found him equal in flavour to a prime turkey.
	Recollections of George Hassing, a prospector[14]

prospectors wanting to get to the West Coast but, due to the difficult terrain and weather, most travellers preferred the sea route.

With growing interest in Westland, the Canterbury Provincial Government invited tenders for surveying contracts along the coastline of their province in 1863. Robert Bain, a twenty-two year-old Australian, had been working as a surveyor for the Canterbury Provincial Government for six years when he was awarded the contract for the section from Arnott Head to Big Bay. His price was £50 per 1000 acres surveyed, which was a rather low figure considering the arduous nature of the country. At this time, however, few Europeans – apart from sealers, whalers and the occasional prospector – had any idea of what the terrain south of Arnott Head was like.

On 28 September 1863 Bain left Port Chalmers with his party of twelve men aboard the schooner *Fawn*, reaching Jackson Bay

The artist Nicholas Chevalier's painting of the junction of the Haast and Burke rivers, from a sketch made by Julius von Haast during his expedition in 1863.
ATL/Te Puna Mātauranga o Aotearoa, F-113533-1/2

> **'It came on to rain as it only can rain on the west coast'**
>
> I found on awakening that the bottom of my tent was flooded and put on my waterproof coat to go and divert the water. Having done so I took off the coat, and found myself covered from head to toe with live maggots. The flies had blown the inside of the sleeves without my being aware of it and it took me two days to get entirely rid of the vermin.
>
> Robert Bain, camping at Cascade Plateau, 2 January 1864[15]

on 12 November. It was a beautiful day when the survey party arrived and presumably the men were optimistic, even though there were large numbers of sandflies. Unused to the biting insects, the men spent the day walking around in waterproof clothing to escape them.

But the trip was to be a catalogue of mishaps. The party was plagued by bad weather. Bain and a small group in a whaleboat were blown northwards fifty miles and spent five days with no blankets or provisions before the wind abated, allowing them to return. A prospector, enlisted to help as survey labour, drowned in the Arawhata River. Finally, when the party had made it down to Martins Bay, the boat they had just embarked on to get to Dunedin was wrecked at the mouth of the Hollyford River, necessitating a five-day walk to Lake Wakatipu. Bain ended up having to petition the provincial government for expenses and the value of equipment he had left at Jackson Bay.[16] The survey from Arnott Head to Jackson Bay was completed in 1864 by John Rochfort, who used Maori assistants and had much better luck.

Gold was discovered on the West Coast in mid 1864, with the main rush happening in early 1865. Periodically there were small rushes to new fields and the Haast district experienced its share of these.

In the summer of 1864-65 there was a gold rush at Jackson Bay and a hundred men were reported to be camped there. An early prospector recorded the *Maid of Erin* arriving from Dunedin and discharging twenty-five tons of cargo, a score of sheep and fifteen passengers. On the same day, the *Aparima* arrived from Invercargill and landed six tons of cargo at 'Cleve's store'. The cutter *Petral* was also at Jackson Bay, about to leave for Invercargill. As usual for South Westland, the rush was short-lived. By December 1866 Jackson Bay was deserted and the store empty. The miners had moved north and were now enthusiastically working the beaches near Haast.[17]

In late January 1867 a rush began at Haast, with the initial find being in a gully three miles south of Haast River. Schooners and steamers entered the river to drop off almost 1500 miners. In the excitement, a town site was surveyed on the south bank of the Haast River and another next to the Okuru River. By August, however, only forty miners remained at the Haast, with other small groups working the beaches down to Jackson

Bay. In November there were sixteen people living near the Arawhata River. The beaches were payable but once the rush was over there were problems getting stores. In December, after three of their number had drowned in the Arawhata, most of the miners were forced to walk through to the nearest town, Okarito, where they arrived, exhausted and starving, fourteen days later. Authorities were alerted to the near starvation of the few miners, including a family, left at the Arawhata and the *West Coast Times* reported that the steamer *Kennedy* was sent down:

Only Mr. and Mrs. Howard and their children and a man named Freshwater were found there. The meeting was a very joyful one on the part of the Howards and their companion. Mrs. Howard especially being quite overpowered by the kind consideration of the ladies who sent down a much needed supply of clothing for herself and children. She desires to return them her grateful thanks. The Howards purchased £50 worth of goods from Mr. McFarline paying for them in gold dust. They were, however,

The survey of a new township, Haast River, 1867	The survey party had commenced laying out a township by staking off a Government Reserve containing an area two acres in extent … Within and about the reserve scores of tents had been erected and a camp formed by the Government party, flanked on either side by the tent of the Resident Magistrate and those erected by the Harbour Master's men … Although at this early stage the Haast River rush was pronounced a 'duffer' by the majority of the new arrivals, these same croakers discovered an intense eagerness to secure building sections in the new township, and when it was known that the business of the day would commence by the survey of the main street, quite two hundred men congregated about the camp, waiting for the surveyor to commence operations. And a motley crowd they were, comprising men of various degrees and much diversity of appearance, including the well-to-do storekeeper, anxious to obtain an advantageous business site, and the ragged street-loafer, who desired to obtain a section, only for the purpose of selling it again to the first bidder. This rush for sections was the only exciting event that took place during my stay at Haast, which, as regards sensational incidents, was singularly unlike a new rush. Old goldfields' residents – veterans in the establishment of new settlements – declared, however, that the scene enacted that morning capped anything of the kind they had ever witnessed, so furious was the struggle to obtain commanding sites. I really pitied Mr Cooper [the surveyor], who was jostled unmercifully by a mob of rowdies, who disputed the possession of every section that was marked, not one of which but was held by half a dozen claimants. In one instance I noticed thirteen pegs round the surveyors mark, and settling disputes as to ownership occupied Mr FitzGerald [Resident Magistrate] nearly the whole of the next day. Not much activity was displayed in building, albeit one or two stores were erected in a primitive fashion, and an enterprising baker constructed an oven, and on Sunday drew his first batch of bread. Special reporter, *West Coast Times*.[18]

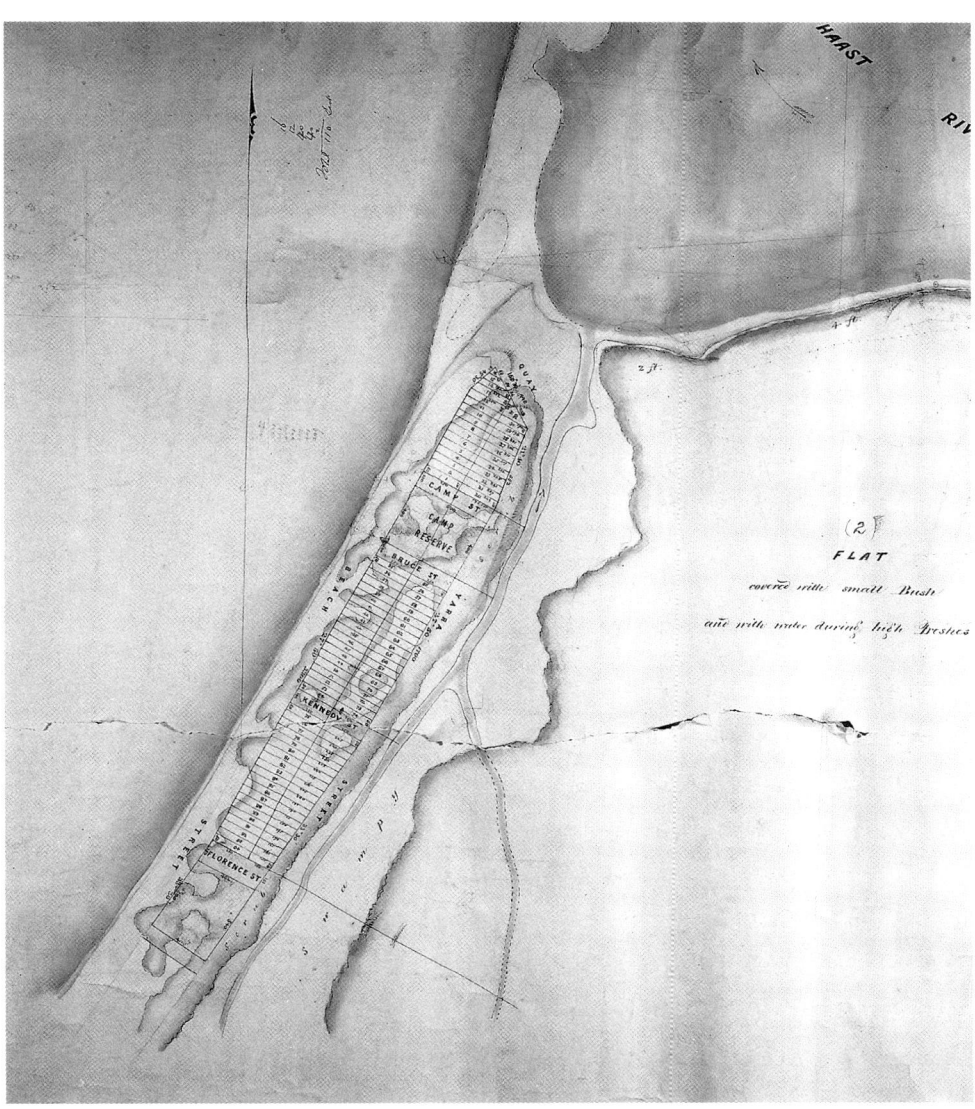

Mr Cooper's survey plan of the new Haast Township, 1867. Department of Lands & Survey, Hokitika District Office records at Archives New Zealand, Christchurch, CH528, Box11, unnumbered

very reticent concerning their earnings, merely stating that moderate wages could be obtained there, but refused to leave the place, not withstanding that a free passage was offered them in the Kennedy.[19]

In September 1873 a rumour began to circulate in Hokitika that prospectors had again found gold in the Haast district. The rumour gained currency when the Okarito warden, Edward Tizard, stated that John Marks and his three mates had walked through to Okarito, deposited thirty-five ounces of gold and applied for a claim north of Haast River. The gold was brought up to Hokitika and displayed in the window of Mr. Brown's

19

jewellery shop, provoking a rush:

> *Although, as we have said, there is really nothing more known about the supposed goldfield than what was stated at the very first, passengers are offering very freely, and it is evident that whether, justifiably or not, a rush of more or less magnitude is setting in. Yesterday both the* Titan *and* Waipara *were speedily filled up with as many passengers as they could take, and the Omeo has been laid on to be despatched to the Haast on her arrival.*[20]

On arriving, prospectors were disappointed to find that they needed to trek about ten miles north and climb over a small range to reach Marks's claim. Returns were meager and most of the men left in disgust. Marks himself didn't think a rush was justified and wrote this letter on 28 September, trying to stop any more people leaving Hokitika for the 'new field':

> *Things are looking very black at present, most of the people returning ... many of them not even having been to the diggings, and the majority having only spent a few hours there. Under the circumstances we must therefore ask you to be kind enough to do all in your power to stop the rush for a time, until something fresh is struck.*[21]

Although a rush was perhaps not justified, there was evidently enough gold to keep Marks and other miners interested in the Haast district. Marks stayed there and set up a store at Haast Beach to supply passing prospectors. In December 1873 he stated that there was another store besides his and that there were about seventy miners in the district.[22] Other people, apart from miners, began to be interested in the area, too.

Some West Coast citizens thought that the southern part of the district needed to be developed, and that a special settlement might provide the impetus for this. The resulting townships would give prospectors a base from which they could venture out to discover the payable goldfields that surely must be there. They looked forward to having railways, roads, fishing industries and large sawmills. In those optimistic colonial times anything seemed possible, even in the most remote part of Westland.

From Haast River south to Jackson Bay.
Department of Conservation

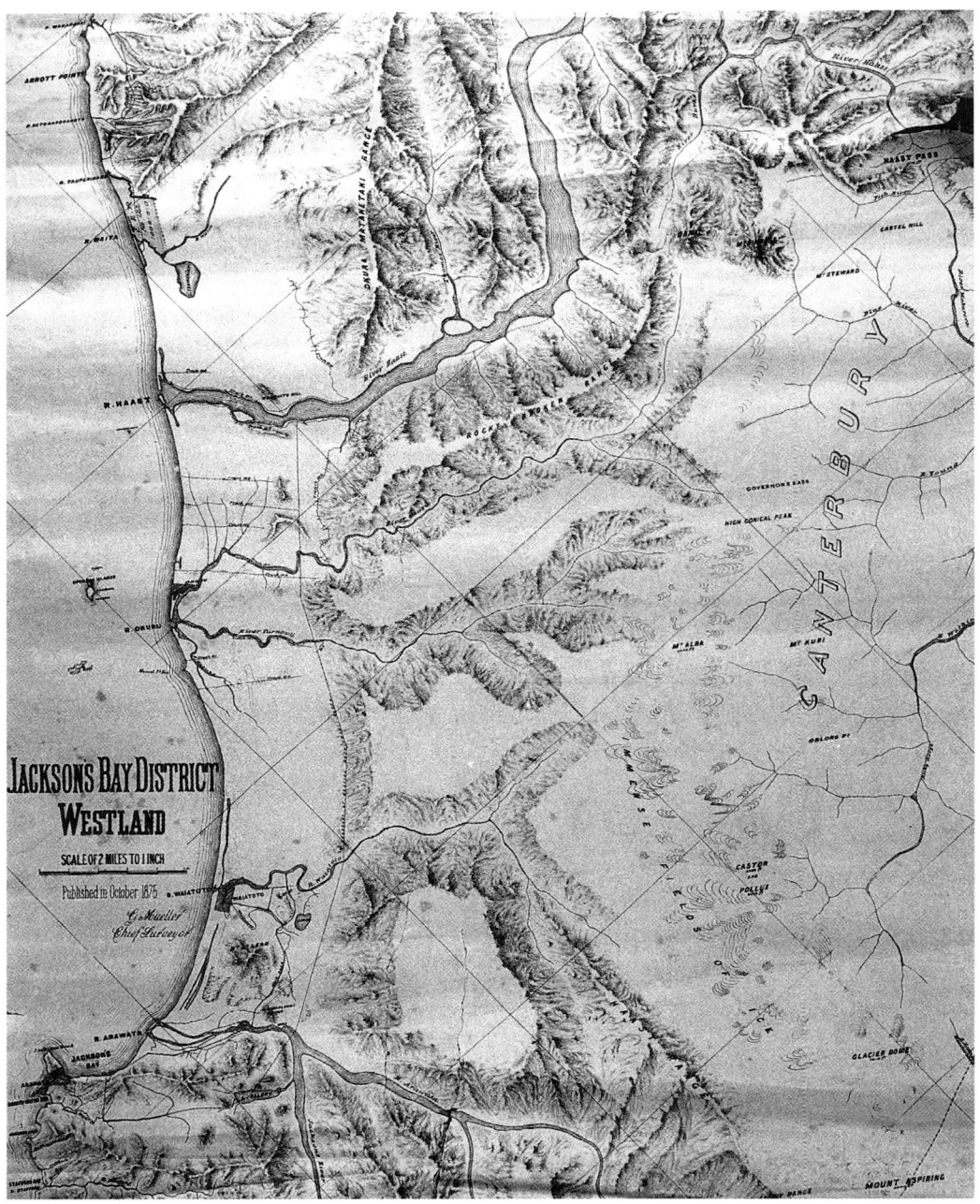

The map of the area selected for a 'Special Settlement', published in 1875.

Department of Lands & Survey, Hokitika District Office records at Archives New Zealand, Christchurch, CH528, Box 5, 2/55

Chapter 2

A Special Settlement at Jackson Bay

Special settlements were introduced in 1870 as a way of 'opening up' new areas of country, by providing a place for some of the many immigrants who were arriving in New Zealand.

The idea of a special settlement in South Westland gained support from some of the leading men of Westland, in particular James Bonar, who became the first Superintendent of Westland when the Westland Provincial Council was formed in January 1874. Bonar successfully lobbied central government. Settlements had already been established at Martins Bay (1870) and Karamea (1874) and the sixty thousand acres of land between Haast and Jackson Bay were seen as an excellent place for farming and timber milling industries. Jackson Bay, with its natural harbour and abundant timber, was thought to be the ideal location for the main town in the district.

Bonar proposed starting with 250 families, who would become the foundation members of a new and prosperous settlement on the south coast. The settlers would initially be drawn from families already resident on the West Coast, but later settlers would be assisted immigrants from Europe. A wharf would be built to enable the development of timber, fishing and brickmaking industries. The government agreed to advance £20,000, part of which would be paid back with proceeds from the sale of land.

James Bonar, the main promoter of the Jackson Bay settlement scheme. He was Superintendent of Westland when the settlement was started in 1875.
West Coast Historical Museum 2492

In November 1874 a delegation proceeded to Jackson Bay to inspect the area and begin laying out sections for the settlers. The party consisted of James Bonar, Gerhard Mueller (chief surveyor), and John Browning (surveyor), who remained at the bay with some men to begin work. The rest of the party, after inspecting Jackson Bay and finding it satisfactory for settlement, proceeded to Okuru. Here they found good land and some miners already resident and planting potatoes. The last stop was the Haast River, where they found more miners.

In late 1874 a pamphlet explaining the conditions for the new settlement at Jackson Bay was printed. Males over the age of sixteen were entitled to take up one ten-acre section (at six shillings per acre per annum) and one fifty-acre block (at three shillings per acre per annum). After seven years of residence they would be granted ownership of the land. Fares to the new settlement would be free and cottages would be provided for families to live in until they had built their own houses. A road was to be made from Jackson Bay to Haast and settlers would be able to obtain half-time work at eight shillings a day for the first two years of settlement. A government store would provide goods at cost price and purchases would be deducted from the men's wages. Duncan Macfarlane was appointed Resident Agent, to oversee the running of the new settlement.

In January 1875 a group of volunteer settlers sailed from Hokitika to their new home at Jackson Bay. There were sixteen families

Opposite:
The survey plan of the Arawata township at Jackson Bay, 1875. Note the large number of 'town sections', some of which were on steep hillsides. The sections were to be sold by auction. Department of Lands & Survey, Hokitika District Office records at Archives New Zealand, Christchurch, CH528, Box 2, 1/105

Duncan Macfarlane, the government's agent at Jackson Bay from 1875 to about 1890.
West Coast Historical Museum

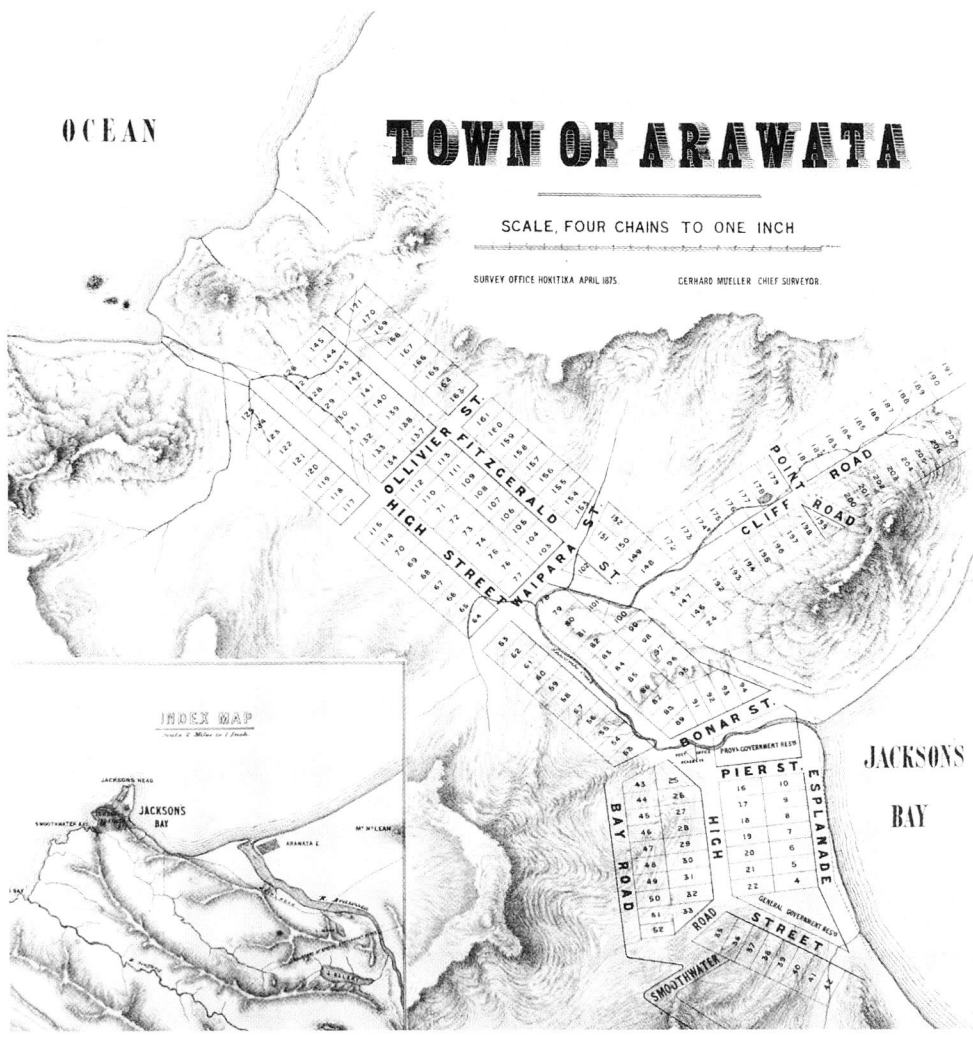

The Great Southern

One of the superintendent's tasks while at Haast was to christen a new water race. At the time, it was the largest to be built on the West Coast by a private group, in this case by David Welsh, John McKenna, Michael Murphy and Michael McKenna. The race carried seventy 'government heads of water' four miles from the Waita River in the north. Twe ve chains of the race were formed by fluming, with the rest being ditches. The shareholders expected to be able to supply 200 men or more with water for mining the Haast Beach. It would be ready in three weeks, the men said, and they would charge £1 per week for water. The superintendent christened the race 'Great Southern', which he thought appropriate as he believed it would 'materially assist in developing the whole of the Southern District'. Little more was heard of the race, and it appears that this adventurous undertaking wasn't quite the roaring success that its builders and shareholders had hoped for.[1]

Three of the earliest settlers at the Jackson Bay Special Settlement: Bridget (née Cox) and Adam Cron and one of their five children. This photo was probably taken shortly before they left Hokitika. They arrived at Jackson Bay with the first group of settlers on 19 January 1875. Courtesy Cliff Cron

and several single men, a total of eighty-one people: 22 men, 13 women and 46 children. The men had been 'carefully selected from a large number of applicants'. The settlers were culturally diverse, being from Scotland, Ireland, England, Germany, Sweden, Denmark and Canada, although all had been living in New Zealand for some time. A second group of 'hand-picked' settlers sailed two weeks later. These people, too, appear to have been in New Zealand for some time and were adaptable and experienced 'colonisers'.[2]

Such was Bonar's enthusiasm that he sent the settlers too early. When they arrived they found that the survey had not been completed, so they were unable to take up any land. Instead, they were employed erecting the government cottages that were to provide temporary homes for themselves and the following waves of intending settlers. Thick bush covered the land and there was no road from the landing place at Jackson Bay to the rural sections. To make things worse, a wharf had not yet been built, hampering the development of any sawmilling or fishing businesses that settlers might have been intending to start. Superintendent James Bonar wrote to the Minister for Immigration, 25 January 1875:

The construction of a jetty is a work of considerable importance, as at present everything has to be landed in boats on a flat stony beach; and with even a moderate swell this would be a work of considerable risk, both to boats and cargo. The expense I do not think will be very heavy, and I propose, therefore, to get plans prepared without delay.[3]

Superintendent Bonar was obviously keen to get the wharf built as soon as possible, but as funding was coming from central government, he needed to obtain authorisation. In February the Minister for Immigration warned that, as only £12,000 remained for expenses connected with the settlement, plans for the wharf must be submitted to him for approval by the Public Works Department before he could authorise any construction. Although Bonar and Macfarlane remained optimistic, this stipulation was a sign of the government's reluctance to spend money on the settlement.

On 6 March 1875 the settlers were able to apply for ten-acre 'suburban' sections at Arawata. The survey, however, was still not complete; the fifty-acre blocks, which some settlers may have preferred to settle on, were not yet available. An un-named settler wrote to the Editor of the *Evening Star*, Hokitika, 9 March 1876:

> *Had we been allowed to continue to work on the road till the fifty-acre sections were open for selection, we should have been in a position to make improvements on these large blocks of land which would benefit us and the country in general. But, instead of this we were compelled by the Resident Agent to build huts and cultivate the ten-acre sections. Now, the result of this … is that we have wasted twelve months' labour on useless land, and have been driven into debt to the amount of from £20 to £60 each, and are now deprived of the means of taking possession of the fifty–acre sections.*

But at least the settlers could begin to erect their own houses and clear some land. By June, twenty-four homes had been built and a 'considerable amount' of land had been cleared in preparation for planting crops in the spring. A fishing company had been started, and many of the settlers were having cattle sent down on the steamer.[4]

In August, Bonar began to send down settlers who had arrived in New Zealand as assisted immigrants. Most came from Germany and Poland, but in July 1876 a group of Italians was sent. Having only recently arrived from their homelands – and, in the case of the Italians, having spent several months in the immigration barracks at Wellington – the settlers found the Haast district something of a shock. Many of them had thought they were being sent to Hokitika, where they hoped to find jobs, and some of the new arrivals refused to settle at Jackson Bay. Two translated accounts of German settlers who had been sent to Jackson Bay, appeared in the *West Coast Times*:[5]

> *Ziglefski, a married woman, said she left her husband at Jackson's Bay. She did not want to stay there. She was not used to such wild looking country. She would not go back … She knew that at Jackson's Bay they got eight shillings a day for three days per week, but they must drink tea three times a day, and likely get in debt. As soon as she went*

ashore she found a woman who had been in service with her, and as soon as the woman saw her she commenced to cry, and asked if she was one of the unfortunate ones to come there. She then told her that they were in debt, and would never come out of it till they died. They did not say that they did not get enough to eat, but clothes were such a price that they could not pay for them. What cost two pence at home cost two shillings there.

Johan Senger, a farm labourer. He went to Jackson's Bay, and was on shore. He was on the mountain. The scrub you couldn't get through and you couldn't look over. He did not see any of the German homesteads, or any of the clearings of the settlers.

Most of the new settlers decided to stay and they worked hard to make the best of their situation. The Italians took up land at Okuru, planning to grow grapes and other fruit trees and to import mulberry trees in order to produce raw silk. Many of the Poles decided to go to Smoothwater Bay, a settlement located several miles south of Jackson Bay.

By March 1877, 367 people were living within the stretch of coastline from Haast River to Smoothwater Bay. Nearly 200 acres of land had been cleared and the settlers had sown grass, planted crops and fruit trees, and made vegetable gardens and flower beds. Most families had a cow to milk and some had pigs and goats. Unfortunately the settlement was plagued by bad weather in its early years, which made growing crops difficult; some were ruined, such as potatoes. In 1878 the district had 259 rainy days, with a total of 134 inches of rain, and suffered severe flooding.[7]

A wharf was desperately needed by the settlers, especially by those planning to develop industries. The Hon. James Macandrew, Minister for Immigration, visited Jackson Bay in March 1878. He instructed Macfarlane to push on with the wharf. However, little progress was made. Despite repeated requests, the government refused to authorise

| Browning's folly – The Smoothwater story | It was not originally intended to settle the Smoothwater area, but when John Browning was surveying the district in 1874 he reported very favourably on Smoothwater Valley. There were, he said, 5000 acres of good land. As a result, the chief surveyor gave instructions for the valley to be laid out in fifty-acre blocks. However, the survey found that the land available was closer to 1600 acres, and that most of it was immediately next to the river and therefore not ideal for settlement. Macfarlane, as resident agent, advised the newly arrived Polish and German settlers not to go there but they were told by another settler that he had told them not to go because he knew there was gold there. The Poles decided to settle at Smoothwater. In March 1877 there were sixty-six people living at Smoothwater in twelve weatherboard houses, with a total of sixteen 50-acre blocks having been taken up. They were to suffer considerably from floods and found the area not particularly suited to agriculture.[6] |

The Macfarlane family's rather grand house at Jackson Bay, c. 1888.
West Coast Historical Museum 6599.

the required expenditure. Piles for the wharf had been erected as far as the water-line when Macfarlane received a telegram from the Under-Secretary of Immigration, saying: 'Engineer and practical persons advise that wharf at Jackson Bay, if erected to stand, would cost two thousand five hundred pounds. Under these circumstances there are no funds available, and work cannot be proceeded with'.[8] The settlers were going to have to survive without the benefit of the industry that a wharf would have facilitated. Thomas Haworth, sawmill owner, wrote to the 1879 Commission of Inquiry:

> *In May last I was induced to erect a sawmill at the Arawata River, Jackson's Bay, on the understanding that the settlers were to own half of the same, and that a jetty for shipping timber was to be erected. The mill was in working order in July, and contracts for cutting timber were let, and a vessel also chartered for two years to convey the timber to market. To my surprise, during the year 1878 Mr. Macfarlane received instructions to stop all works in connection with the jetty, of which one and a-half chains were then completed. As I was fully under the impression that the jetty was to be completed when I entered upon the speculation, the stoppage of this work has entailed on me a very heavy loss … unless the jetty is completed I shall be a very heavy loser by my venture. On the other hand, I am quite prepared to go on working the mill when there is a jetty, as I am quite satisfied that the quantity and quality of the timber is first class, and equal to any bush in New Zealand, and will find employment for settlers for the next ten years.[9]*

In its early days the district appears to have been marred by some petty squabbles, which were exacerbated by cultural and

language difficulties and personality differences between Macfarlane and some of the residents. Macfarlane thought some of the settlers lazy, while those settlers, on the other hand, thought that he was showing favouritism to a selected few.

Mary (née Spillane) and Andrew Nolan and children at their new house at Okuru c. 1885.
Courtesy Bill Nolan

From January 1878 the government no longer ran the store at Arawata township, having tendered it out to John Marks, who was running stores at Haast and Okuru. The grievances appear to have arisen when Macfarlane attempted to collect some of the money settlers owed to the government store, money they could ill afford to pay. On a salary of £300 per annum, he may not have fully realised the difficulties that the settler families were experiencing. For example, Joseph Heveldt, Erasmus Nisson and Andrew Nolan, each with a wife and at least three children, averaged about £50 per annum over the three years.[10] Disputes at the settlements culminated in a commission of inquiry in 1879, which exonerated Macfarlane and recommended that a wharf be built to encourage industries which would provide jobs and income for the settlers. The recommendation was never acted upon.

Many people were leaving the settlements. Most of the Poles, realising that Smoothwater would never be a success, moved to Taranaki in the North Island in late 1878 and early 1879. The Italians, who had initially held high hopes for agriculture in the Okuru district, left in 1879, as did other settlers who despaired of ever making their land pay. Those who remained had taken up fifty-acre blocks and were making some sort of living from farming. The Arawata township and Arawata settlement emptied out as settlers based themselves at the Waiatoto, Okuru and Turnbull rivers. In late 1883, a surveyor named Barron visited the area; he reported only two families at Arawata township, while there were five at Arawata settlement, eight at the Waiatoto, and nine at Okuru.[11]

In 1887 a reporter visited Jackson Bay and noted,

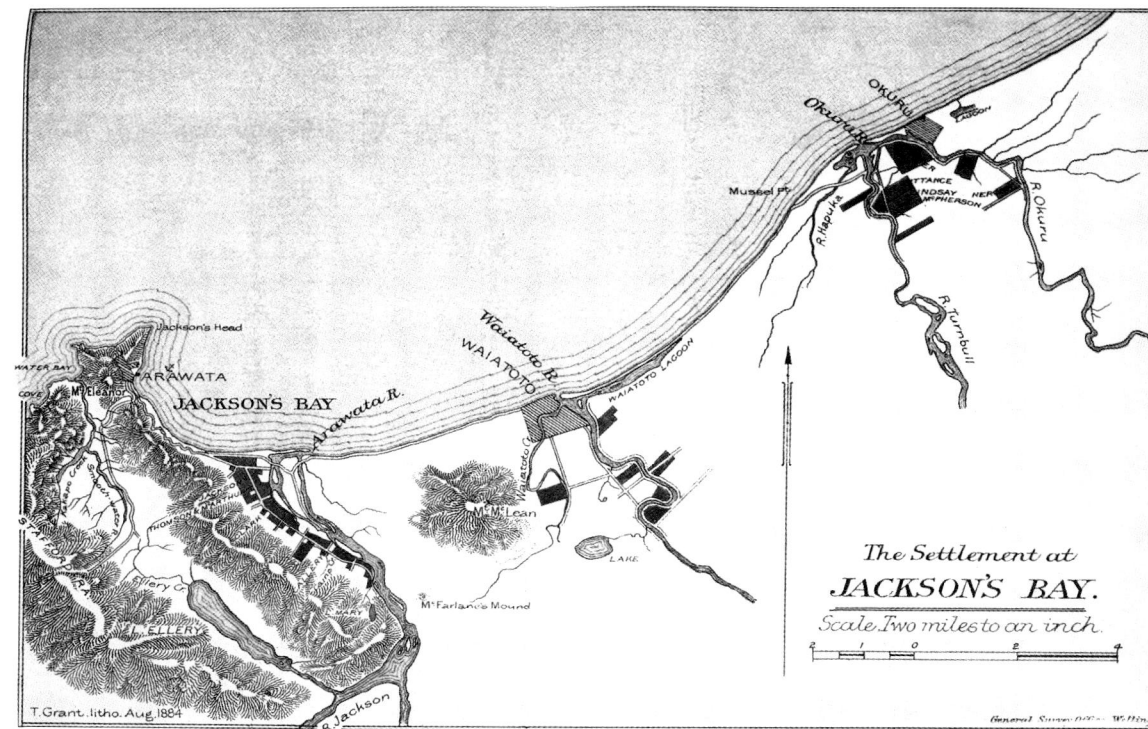

The Settlement at
JACKSON'S BAY.
Scale Two miles to an inch.

An 1884 map of the Jackson Bay to Okuru district showing some of the rural sections which were still occupied. Barron, the surveyor responsible for the map, did not visit the Waiatoto settlement – hence some names are missing.
AJHR, Vol. 1. Session 2, C-1 App. 5, p. 76.

The buildings consist of the Resident Magistrate's pretentious dwelling, built and furnished by the Government at an expense of over a thousand pounds, a courthouse, a lock-up tumbling to decay, a disused schoolhouse in a like condition, Mr Robinson's Hotel, a smithy pro bono publico, Mr Lindsay's cottage, and a deserted hut.[12]

In this remote locality, with paid work for the road-makers petering out, the remaining settlers struggled to make any sort of income at all. Butter was made and packaged for tearooms and bakeries in Hokitika, but once again the problem was getting the produce to the market. If the steamer was late or didn't call, the butter would spoil. Cattle could be sold, but first it was necessary to walk them along bush tracks for about 130 miles to Whataroa, the nearest market. In general, families had enough to live on, eating the occasional cattle beast or sheep, shooting birds and keeping large vegetable gardens, but they had very little money to spare.

For the next fifty years communication with the outside world remained essentially the same. Mail arrived fortnightly via the mailman and his horse, and the steamer called every two or three months with stores. In about 1910 an unreliable telephone service was established, and from the 1930s the people of the Haast district could listen to the wireless. A trip out of the district usually meant several days of horse riding, either

A crowd at a day of horse racing at the Okuru, c. 1909. Families would have travelled from both north and south of Okuru in order to attend.
From the booklet Jackson Bay Centenary 1874–1974

via the track through the Haast Pass to Wanaka or north to the Fox and Franz Josef glaciers on the Paringa cattle track.

       The big breakthrough for the residents was the arrival in the district of an aeroplane in 1931. In 1934 Bert Mercer and Air Travel New Zealand started a regular service to Haast and Okuru. Suddenly the world opened up. Fresh bread was flown in, newspapers arrived on the day they were printed, and medical emergencies were less threatening when the sick and injured could be flown out to hospital. Locals took to air travel with gusto and it is likely that during the 1930s, per head of population, more people in the district had flown in an aeroplane than in any other area of New Zealand.

A group of travellers at the Iron Hut on the Haast to Paringa cattle track.
Alexander Turnbull Library/Te Puna Matauranga o Aotearoa, F- 18973-1/4

Myrtle, Ivy and Jack Cron with Bert Mercer at the Haast airstrip c. 1940.
Courtesy of Paul Beauchamp Legg

Bert Mercer, the pilot who began an air service to the isolated settlements of South Westland in 1934.
West Coast Historical Museum 7405

In late 1937 government approval was finally given for a wharf at Jackson Bay. The intention was (once again) to develop the district, and as part of this plan roads were to be built from Jackson Bay to Haast. Suddenly the bay was a hive of activity. A camp for one hundred men was built, and of necessity it was self-contained. Buildings included a bakery, hospital, post office, and a wireless room; even a local newspaper was produced.

The contract for the wharf was let to Rope Construction Limited, who used a steam pile-driver mounted on a barge to bang the piles in. Within a year it had been built and was in almost constant use, much of the cargo being machinery for road-building. Smaller camps were established at various points along the road from Jackson Bay to Haast.

Meanwhile men were working on the Haast Pass road and the road south from the glaciers. The outbreak of World War Two slowed down work and many of the men and buildings at Jackson Bay were moved to Haast to begin work on an aerodrome. The Haast aerodrome, which was part of the national defence plan, was completed in August 1944.

After the war, the finishing touches were made to the road from Jackson Bay to Haast. Work then focused on both the Haast Pass road and the road north. The road to Otago via the pass was opened on 12 November 1960 with due ceremony. At long last, the district was connected to the outside world by a road. The district would never be the same again, but locals heartily welcomed the change. In 1965 the road to the glaciers and Hokitika was completed: the district was now on a through road.

The new Public Works Department village at Jackson Bay before the wharf was built, c. 1937. West Coast Historical Museum 6150

Building the wharf at Jackson Bay. Rope Construction began building the wharf in April 1938 and finished ten months later. West Coast Historical Museum 7671

The departing road-workers left a gap in the community that was soon filled by people moving to the district to work in the saw-mill opened by Carters in the 1960s. During each spring the population swelled with an influx of people wanting to catch whitebait. The combination of road access and a wharf now meant that fishermen began to base themselves at Jackson Bay. The long-awaited 'Progress' had finally arrived.

The opening of the road from Haast to Wanaka via Haast Pass in 1960.
Courtesy of Paul Beauchamp Legg.

Joseph and Dorothea Heveldt with their sons (left to right)
Joseph, Frank, Henry, John, c. 1900.
Courtesy of Francis Henry Heveldt

Chapter 3

Residents of Arawata
1875–1925

Heveldt Family

Joseph and Dorothea Heveldt (née Zovisch) set sail from Hamburg, Germany, in April 1875, arriving in Wellington on 11 July 1875. Joseph was thirty-six and Dorothea twenty-nine. They were not assisted immigrants, having paid the full fare for themselves and their four children, two of whom were from Joseph's first marriage. A week after their arrival the family left Wellington with a group of other immigrants for the new settlement at Jackson Bay.

The Heveldts settled on one of the rural sections at the Arawata settlement and the size of the family increased to twelve with the arrival of a further six children, all born at Arawata. Joseph did road-building work whenever it was available to help support his large family, but times must have been very hard for them.

Joseph's eldest surviving son, Albert, drowned in the Arawhata River in 1881 at the age of eighteen. His body was retrieved by Mary Nolan (née Spillane), who, as there were no men around, stripped off to her underclothes and dived into the pool to get it. Afterwards Mary was much censured by some of the other women for being indecent. In 1892 Joseph and Dorothea lost a five-year-old son and in 1901 another son, James, died at the age of twenty.

The family nearly shifted to Dannevirke in the late 1870s but Joseph was persuaded to stay on – there would be plenty of work, he was told, when the road was opened through the Haast Pass. They lived at Arawata until about 1900. Joseph and Dorothea then shifted to Hokitika and one of their youngest sons, August, who had been born at Arawata in 1883, continued living at the family home until about 1925 when he left the district. Two of Joseph and Dorothea's sons were inter-viewed about their childhood at Arawata by Radio New Zealand in 1961.

Frank Heveldt
1874–1964

Frank arrived in the Arawata settlement as a fifteen-month-old baby. In 1902 he married Mary Nolan, with whom he had attended Arawata School. The couple ran the Forks Hotel, near Okarito, for many years before retiring to Hokitika.

The settlement had started. We were in the first batch of Germans, practically. There were a few before us but not many. The land that was there, there was a road formed and then ten-acre sections cut off. There was a creek running through it and when there was a flood, the creek overflowed over the road and everywhere and left you in water. The first place we were in, it was only a bungie maimai [ponga hut] with a slab roof, the floor was made of logs, dragged in and squared up a bit and flattened out. We'd be up in the loft getting baggage off the floor. There was an old chap across the road from us, McGlashan, an old ship's carpenter, and he had a step-son there, grown up. They used to piggy-back us out to Granny's, as we called it. We were wishing there was a flood every day of the week because we'd get a bit of bread over there. We wouldn't get it every day at home; we hadn't got it.

My father did road-work mainly. The main road going from Jackson Bay leading right up to the end of the settlement. It was formed, making it about twelve to fourteen foot wide, but it was never used – it was just a path.

A lot of them [German and Polish settlers] got out of it. They could see there was nothing there and they went to Dannevirke and got sections there, and they done all right. My dad went up there and he had a section ready for us to go on to. He came back and was selling up when they put men on the first track over the Haast and he was persuaded to stop. Because once this Haast road got over, oh there'd be work there and it would be a wonderful place.

It was all under water, all the sections. They tried to farm them, they chopped bush off and burnt it up but it was clay stuff and it wouldn't grow anything. Except you'd get patches along the riverbed, but then again when the river was high it would bank over and that was no good. It was an awful place.

The folk that opened up it up they would have known – surely to goodness they had the brains to know – that it wasn't any good. It was run by the government. All the damaged cargo was sent down there, and it was take it or leave it. I remember going in, my mother and I, to get a fifty [lb bag] of flour and there was a lot of it on the counter. Adam Cron – he was running it for the government. Anyway we got this fifty of flour, and you wouldn't know it was flour – it was just a big heap of weevils. If it wasn't for that I wouldn't remember anything about it, but it was seeing these weevils rolling, that impressed my mind. We paid top price for it. We had to carry the stuff out six miles on our backs, there were no horses. When we tried to bake it – well, you might as well go out there and get the mud out of the gutters, there would be just as much rising in it as there was in that flour. It wasn't flour at all, it was just weevils and we had to take it or leave it.

Women had a hard time because the men were away working. They would send cash, and by the time they had paid for their own tucker there wasn't such a great lot left, the men would practically half starve themselves on the job doing it. There was a store in the bay at the time, run by the government and, as I say, all the rubbish that they couldn't sell up here [in Hokitika], they'd sell down there. It was cruel, cruel.[1]

John Heveldt
1879–1961
John and his wife, Maude (née Sellars), had three children. John was widowed after only nine years of marriage.

Their tools were a cross-cut saw, and an axe and a hammer. That was about all they had, and they all built homes in a few days. They had to get their provisions from Jackson Bay, about ten miles, and they had to carry them all on their backs. My father and mother used to carry them and I've known my mother to carry a fifty [lb bag] of flour on

her back for about ten miles. All the people were in the same boat.

The settlers were mixed people but the majority of the ones in the Arawata settlement were Poles but there were some Germans among them, and some Scots and some Irish – but not so many Irish. There was no minister, there was no church at all, but I can remember Polish men, of a Sunday they'd get together and sing their Polish hymns.

There was a cemetery and there is fourteen buried in it, as far as I know. I have three brothers buried there. There is one grave that nobody knows except myself. It is outside the cemetery, about two chains I think, buried there before the cemetery was started. I must tell you about this. There is a little river in behind Jackson Bay called the Smoothwater River. The Polish people were dumped in there, about seven miles, I think, from Jackson Bay. It is a forest of large white birch trees [kaihikatea] and they were supposed to carve their homes out there. They went in with an axe and a saw. Those poor people knew nothing at all about felling trees. This one man started to chop a large tree near his house, and of course he went round and round it, chopping round and round it, and he felled the tree on the house and killed his wife. I think that must be the grave that's outside Arawata cemetery.

There were plenty fish in the river. I never saw so many herring as was in the Arawhata River, and flounders. But we never

The Heveldt family home at Arawata in 1926, shortly after the departure of the township's last permanent resident, Gus Heveldt.
Otago Witness, *22 June 1926.*

Tragedy at Smoothwater

To Mr E. Patten, Esq., Hokitika

Sir, I have the honor to report that on the 29th June a settler's wife at Smoothwater met with her death through the falling of a tree on his house. The circumstances were as follows:- The husband of the deceased was engaged cutting down a tree in the neighbourhood of his house, and he told his wife to keep outside until such time as the tree was down, as it might fall on the house. She expressed great fear about the tree, but, for some unaccountable reason, just before the tree was cut through, she went inside, and before she could get out she was caught by the falling tree and was killed on the spot. A child that she had with her was unhurt. I held an inquest on the body, when the jury returned a verdict of accidental death. The accident threw quite a gloom over the settlement.

I have, &c.,
D. Macfarlane
Resident Agent.

Rosalie Witski was thirty-five when she was killed in June 1877. From Poland, Rosalie had arrived at Jackson Bay with her husband and three children in July 1876. Her husband and children left the district soon after Rosalie's death.[2]

got them because the poor old men never knew anything about fishing or even shooting. We could have lived well on fish but we couldn't get them. Jackson Bay was teaming with groper, terakihi, and all sorts of rock fish and crayfish but we very seldom got one because the men were not fishermen and they were that poor that I don't think they would have had enough money to buy a hook if they had a place to buy it, but I don't believe they had a place to buy a hook.

There were pigeons in millions and there were wekas, millions I suppose, thousands anyhow. We very seldom got one because the old hands didn't know anything about catching or shooting a bird. Small birds, they were in millions and millions. All the most beautiful birds you could ever look at. If you went out of a morning, early, you couldn't hear one another talk unless you were close together because of the song of the birds. But our government brought the weasel into the country, and there's all our beautiful birds gone.

There was a pub in Jackson Bay in the early times and I can remember the man that owned it quite well, Charley Robinson. He was an Englishman. One night a creek broke through at the back of the pub. About midnight him and his son, who was about twelve or thirteen years of age, went up to turn that creek. A big slip come off the hill and buried the boy and he is still buried there.[3]

Robinson Family

The Robinson family ran a hotel in Jackson Bay in the 1880s and suffered the loss of a child.

A sad fatality, it will be remembered, occurred here last Christmas twelve months, when Mr. Robinson lost a promising boy of 14 by a great landslip, which did more or less damage to all the houses and gardens at the settlement at the head of the bay, not excepting Mr. Macfarlane's house, which is the farthest from the slip in the direction it took. The story as told to us by Mr. Robinson after tea that evening of the loss of his boy is a pitiful one. Torrents of rain had been falling for many hours, and, on this particular night, Mrs. Robinson drew the attention of her husband to the fact that water was coming in at the back door of the hotel. There was a water-race leading from a creek in the gully of the range at the back of the house by which a constant supply of water was obtained for domestic purposes, and this was running over into the house. The night was dark and the rain heavy, but Mr. Robinson essayed to go out and turn the water off into the creek, and called his son Charles (his namesake) to go with him to hold a lamp. Obedient to his father's commands, out in the dark, dark night the boy went – went to meet his untimely death, and alas his grave too! Whilst they were proceeding to turn or in the act of turning the water off, a roar like thunder came from the hills and gully behind the settlement, and in a moment Mr. Robinson was carried off his legs by a landslip – a moving sea of earth. He succeeded, however, in keeping his head above the water and debris by clinging to the branches of a big tree that was being carried along by the wave of earth and water, and having regained his feet, his first thought was for his son. "Charley!" he cried, "are you there?" "Yes dada! I'm here," replied the boy. Seconds were like minutes then, and again the father called "Charley! Are you there?" There was no response this time. Again and again Charley was called, but no reply came, and the father scrambled along and into his home hoping his son had made his way there before him. What his feelings were when he found that his boy had not returned, none but a parent's heart can imagine. Diligent search was made by the friends and neighbours, but to this day the remains of the poor boy lie buried in the big slip – maybe on the site of his own father's garden a foot or two from the surface, or, possibly with twelve to fourteen feet of earth upon them, yards from the place where the voice of the dutiful son was last heard. Although so many months have passed away since the sad calamity took place, the father's voice faltered several times during his narration of the sad story of his bereavement, and he was compelled to leave the fireside and room as often to gain his self-possession.

The *Kumara Times* reporter on a visit to Jackson Bay in 1888.[4]

Jackson Bay after the slip of 1887. On the left is the government store and Duncan Macfarlane's house is at the right. The Robinson's hotel is out of view but would have been to the right of the photo. West Coast Historical Museum 6600

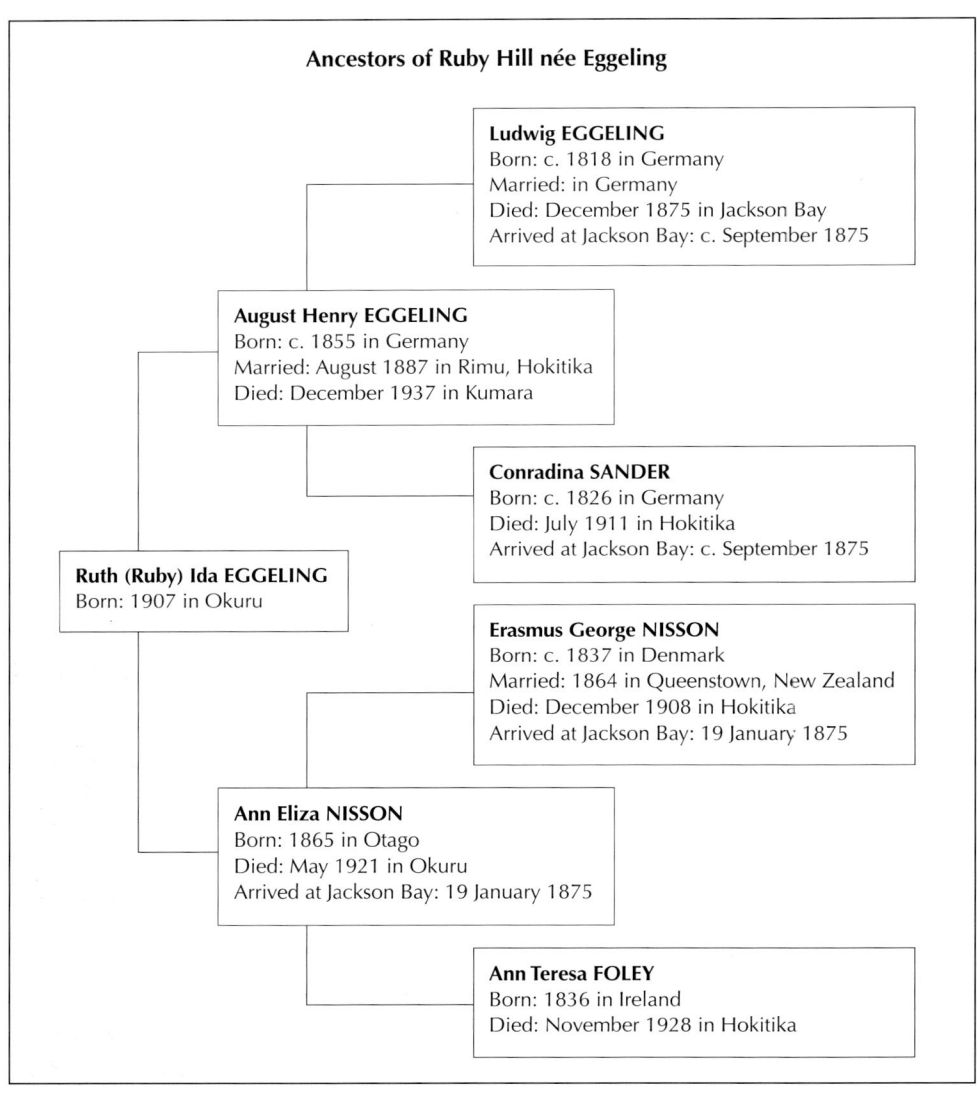

Ancestors of Ruby Hill née Eggeling

Ludwig EGGELING
Born: c. 1818 in Germany
Married: in Germany
Died: December 1875 in Jackson Bay
Arrived at Jackson Bay: c. September 1875

August Henry EGGELING
Born: c. 1855 in Germany
Married: August 1887 in Rimu, Hokitika
Died: December 1937 in Kumara

Conradina SANDER
Born: c. 1826 in Germany
Died: July 1911 in Hokitika
Arrived at Jackson Bay: c. September 1875

Ruth (Ruby) Ida EGGELING
Born: 1907 in Okuru

Erasmus George NISSON
Born: c. 1837 in Denmark
Married: 1864 in Queenstown, New Zealand
Died: December 1908 in Hokitika
Arrived at Jackson Bay: 19 January 1875

Ann Eliza NISSON
Born: 1865 in Otago
Died: May 1921 in Okuru
Arrived at Jackson Bay: 19 January 1875

Ann Teresa FOLEY
Born: 1836 in Ireland
Died: November 1928 in Hokitika

Chapter 4

'You grew up very innocent'

Ruby Hill

Ruby (née Eggeling) was the oldest person I interviewed, having been born at Okuru in 1907. She was the youngest of the ten children born to August Eggeling and Annie (née Nisson). She was just about to turn ninety-one when I visited. She was fascinating to listen to, recalling events and people from a decade earlier than most of the other interviewees. She left Haast in about 1923 and, after working around the South Island for sixteen years, married and settled in the Grey Valley area. Ruby now lives in Ngahere (twenty-five kilometres inland from Greymouth) near her five children.

my father

My father came out from Germany. He was only a boy – I think about nine or ten when he came out. He was in Australia for a couple of years, and from Australia he came down to Jackson Bay. He went to a little place called the Waiatoto and lived in a little hut for a while. Then he shifted up and they built a house at Okuru. He put the rest of his life in down there. He took up road work when he arrived and he worked all over the different places. He used to work over the Haast way quite a bit and come home only on the weekends.

Ruby Hill (née Eggeling).
Courtesy, Mary Savage

my mother

When my mother was having a baby they had to come from the Waiatoto right up to Okuru and across the river up to Mrs McPherson's, she used to deliver the babies. Anyway on her way up she went into labour and she never made it. She had the baby halfway between Waiatoto and Okuru, on the roadside. It would have been quite an experience for her.

She was a very hard-working woman; she used to do a lot of work outside. We milked the cows, just for our own use, and she used to milk in the mornings and milk at nights. She used to make the butter and all that sort of thing. It was a very different life to what any of us live now.

She was a great worker and looked after things. My father used to come home on weekends and help around the place. I was the youngest – there was quite a space in-between the last four of us. There was three years of a space in-between us. But the older ones were a lot older than what I was. From when I was born two of the older ones were never home – they were away out working. You don't get to know them the same when you are living away from them. My eldest sister worked at the mental hospital in Hokitika, that is Seaview. It was always called the mental hospital at that time. Both my oldest sisters worked there.

my brothers

My two oldest brothers, they were both away to the war. One got home, the other one got killed at the war. Henry, he got killed. I must have been only about nine when my brother was killed, and times then were very different to what they are now. Children were all sent outside – not to be inside listening to the conversations – and you didn't know what

The Eggeling family of Okuru in 1909. Back (left to right): George, Johanna, Henry, Anne, Charlie. Front: Grace, Annie, Ruby, August, Dick. From the booklet Jackson Bay Centenary 1874–1974

was going on. Today they are more grown up because they are told more, but you got told very very little, as far as I can remember, with our parents. You grew up very innocent really.

Another brother, he got drowned. There had been a big flood in the Haast River and he had to cross it. He had trouble with his ears and a resident up there tried to whistle and stop him, to tell him not to go, but anyway he didn't hear it. Apparently, from what I could always gather, his horse got into quicksand and he must have been thrown off or something, but they never ever found his body. I think I might have been only about five. The only thing I can really remember about him was that he gave me a brooch. I was very very little then and I must have been very taken with this brooch. That's more or less the last thing that I could remember of him, was him giving me this brooch. I don't know whether it was a birthday or what it was – it must have been something. I always appreciated that but I was very little then; I might not have even been five.

Christmas

Birthdays weren't really recognised then. The same with Christmas – we really only got a new dress. Every Christmas we got a new dress and a new hat. Hats were worn if you went to Sunday school or anywhere – you had to have your hat on. Christmas was always the most wonderful time of the year. All our groceries and that sort of thing came from Hokitika by boat down to Okuru, and of course it was a wonderful day for everybody to go to the boat and get all their groceries and things off the boat. At Christmas time we always got a great big tin of lollies. They were those boiled lollies that you never ever see now. We used to think it was wonderful to get all this stuff that you'd never see the rest of the year.

They always cooked a Christmas dinner. I can remember there was always plum duff, I know that. At that time there was money put into the plum pudding and everyone was wanting plenty of pudding so they could get the money.

Sundays

Sunday was definitely [a day off]. My mother wouldn't even sew a button on a blouse on a Sunday. It was a real day. I can always remember we had to put all our shoes out the night before. We polished our own shoes and they had to be polished every Saturday. Everything was done on a Saturday – you done nothing on Sunday, except the dinner. There was no church, they went to the hall. Mother was a Catholic, my father was Church of England. We went to church with Mother and he always made sure we went off with her, and he went to his own church when his minister was there to go to.

We lived on one side of the river and everything else was across on the other side of the river. We either had to cross the river on horseback, or if it was high tide we had a boat and my father used to always take us across in the boat. On this particular day – it must have been round about Christmas time because we had just got new hats and new dresses — my father had taken us across the river to Sunday school and he'd come back to meet us, to bring us home. On the way home, we were on horseback, three of us on the one horse. I'd picked up some stones on the beach before I'd got on the horse and I said to my father, 'Can I throw the stones in the river when we are crossing?' And he said, 'Yes.' But instead of throwing it behind the horse I threw it in front of horse, and the horse swung right round and the three of us went off into the river! Our new hats went floating down the river — I think that was the biggest heartbreak.

school
It was one of the Cuttances that taught us at school. We were at a bit of a handicap where we were; if it was high tide in the morning we had to cross the river by boat and one of the older ones would row the boat across and put us off and we'd run away to school. When school came out in the evening, if the tide was out, they would have to come over on a horse and pick us up. If the river was high enough they would pick us up in a boat. If there was a very big flood in the river we would have to have the day home, we couldn't go to school and we got quite a bit of that one way and another, but we were always made to learn at home what we were supposed to be learning at school.

I must have only been about eleven when I finished the last of my schooling. We had very, very poor schooling at that time down there. There was no teachers down there. There was only older girls from other families that taught schooling but actually they had had very little education themselves. I don't think high school was ever thought about as far as we were concerned — you only went through to standard five or something like that. After I finished school I worked at home, that's all you could do, there was nothing else to do.

homelife
Oh yes, the bread was all baked at home. The bread was all made and cooked in a camp oven over a big open fire. We had an orchard down there and we had many different kinds of apples. We had kinds that you never ever see today. Mother used to make jam, nothing else. They had their rhubarb and they made apple and rhubarb jam, and rhubarb and fig jam, and all that sort of thing. I can remember that instead of bottling it that they had stone jars and that jam was put into those. As far as cakes went I don't think they ever done much baking. I can remember going home from school and mother was always buttering bread and putting jam on it for us to have a piece after we got home from school. I don't think I could even look at rhubarb jam today.

I don't ever remember taking much else but bread and jam to school. Look, I wouldn't give anyone bread and jam, but I don't think they had anything else to give us. We always had plenty to eat but there was no variety or anything. It was always the same sort of thing – corned beef and plenty of that sort of thing. They cured their own ham and cured their own bacon. I know they made sausages, I can still see them hanging up in strings in the smoke house.

We had our own vegetable garden. They ran cattle. Every year there was a beast killed and they had pigs. I can always remember them killing pigs. And we had hens. They used to make their own brine to corn the meat and I can remember what they used to call the smoke house. They'd go out and catch eels and smoke them and hang them up in the smoke house, and they would smoke their own sausages and different things like that. I often wonder now, I don't think I could ever go back to the same living. It was so isolated. The boat would come down, I think it was only every six months, and once a fortnight a horseman used to come down and he brought the papers and the mail.

I can remember going out. We always went by boat. Your only way of getting home again was by riding a horse because the boat didn't go very often. We started off riding the horses from the Franz Josef, and then after that they got a road put through to Fox Glacier – but of course that was many years later. In the earlier stages it was always from the Franz Josef.

Ruby Eggeling aged about thirteen, c.1920.
Courtesy of Mary Savage

our neighbours

We always had to cross the river to get to them. There were people by the name of McPherson. Well, old Mrs McPherson – she taught me to knit. We used to go up and see her but you had to walk all the way, perhaps a few miles, but you would think nothing of it. There were people by the name of Cuttances – well, there was a family of them, they were our closest neighbours, I think – no, there was Cowans, they were closer but there was no children there. The Cuttance children and us played together. Sunday was about the only day that they'd let us go and play together.

Mrs McPherson

She was quite an aged woman, an elderly woman. She seemed to be able to turn her hand to anything. As children we all knew that she used to smoke the pipe and of course at that time us children thought it was a terrible thing but she would never let you see, if anyone was coming she would always get away out of it but we could smell the smoke. She was a lovely person.

If anybody wanted to come over to our place, unless they had a way of getting over themselves, we used to have to go and ferry them over in the boat. They would come to the river – well, there was no telephones or anything to ring up and say we're coming will you meet us.

Mrs McPherson survives a fire

Mr J. Collyer writing from Okuru says: –
On Monday 29th April at 4 a.m. Mrs McPherson was aroused from her sleep by the light and noise of fire crackling. She immediately secured her young child about two years of age and ran out of the house with her other two children, calling out at the same time. She then left the young child to the care of her eldest boy, who is about six or seven years of age and commenced saving what she could, nobody arriving in time to assist her. Although she tried to induce her little boy to call the neighbours, he was too timid, so the house and everything was burnt to the ashes. Mrs McPherson was burned about the arm and foot while endeavouring to save her box full of wearing apparel in which she did not succeed; in fact not a stitch of clothing was saved, only a little bedding. Mr McPherson left the house the evening before. He is working about eight miles away, coming home every Saturday evening and returning to his work on Sunday evening. The fire is supposed to have been caused by a spark from the chimney as there was no fire in the grate when Mrs McPherson went to bed. Mr McPherson is well known as a hard working, industrious man. Mrs McPherson and family are at present kindly housed with Mr and Mrs W. Cuttance, where she is receiving every attention that can possibly be given. Her arm and foot are improving.

West Coast Times 15 May 1889 p. 2

They would come and they would cooee out as loud as they could yell and hope that we would hear them calling, which we always seemed to do. We'd go down and take the boat out and go over and get them, and they'd come over and spend perhaps an afternoon with us and then away again.

There was a family of Nissons, they were the only relations we had down there. They lived a long way from us too, but we used to go and see them or they'd come and see us. My mother was a Nisson, her brother was George Nisson and there was quite a family of them. They lived on the same side of the river as us.

recreation

We used to have evenings playing cards. It was always on a Saturday night. They might come to our place one night, and the next Saturday night we might go to someone else's place and so on all round. It was always quite an evening really. I think everybody tried to see who could make the best supper and put on a real evening.

On Sundays we used to often go down to the sea-beach. We didn't live very far from the sea and there were lots of rocks. In the season we used to go down and pick mussels, and take a kerosene tin and bread and butter and have a picnic. We'd light a fire and boil the mussels in a kerosene tin which was always very nice. Other times we used to go riding on our horses, down on the beaches or somewhere.

Everybody was friends to one another. It was such a small community. There was only the McPhersons, McBrides, Cuttances, Cowans and Nolans – oh, and the Nissons. That's all the families that were down there; there was no more in the time that I lived down there.

They had sports days and men used to do chopping and there was always running for the children. They usually had a lolly scramble for the children. That was always quite an exciting day for all the people in the district. Usually after the sports day there was always the dance at night. It used to go right on till daylight, the dancing never stopped till it was well into the early morning. You saw very few drunks or anything like that, very very few. I don't ever remember seeing them, and of course when I lived down there it would be a disgrace if you drank. Now women do the same as men do really, but at that time it was a disgrace to see a woman have a glass of beer or anything.

People coming from the Haast down to Okuru – before they could get to Okuru they had to cross a river. My sister Johanna, she had a boat and she would ferry them across. She used to row people backwards and forwards and was quite capable of doing it. I suppose we were all brought up to do that sort of thing. She used to spend a lot of time fishing.

Oh, look – the whitebait! You can't believe it, but you know you'd go out and you'd just catch it by the kerosene-tinful. I suppose there is more people fishing for it now, but there's not the whitebait about like there was then. For a long time it was just buried in the gardens. After that, Din Nolan set up a factory at Okuru. They used to bring whitebait in from up the Haast and different places just on packhorse.

health

I had my teeth out at the Haast – oh, there was about five or six of us down there. Teeth were never looked after really at that time. I had all my teeth out on the top except two eye-teeth, two great big eye-teeth. I can always remember that, I thought it was terrible, these two great big tusks there. There was three or four of us had the same thing done, had all our teeth out. He came over from Wanaka or somewhere over there and he stayed at the Haast and that's where he took our teeth out. We rode up to the Haast on horseback and had our teeth out and came home the next day, and that was ten miles. It was six or nine months before you were allowed to get [false] teeth in. When they were fitting mine they took the two eye-teeth out. I was only young – I think I must have been about ten when I had my teeth out.

What I can remember was just having a doctor's book. They used to look up the symptoms in the book and treat you that way. I remember every Saturday we were lined up – and I think every family was the same – for a dose of epsom salts or senna tea – it was the most putrid stuff – and castor oil. It would be one of the three things, you could take your choice what you wanted. Maybe that's what kept us all well!

Mother had appendicitis. They were going to take her out but there was bad weather or something, and they couldn't shift her. So there was two doctors in Hokitika and they both came down and they did the operation on the kitchen table. She came out of the operation quite well, but it was her kidneys packed up, and that's how it was she died. I was thirteen.

I don't really remember [my mother's funeral]. I remember they took us into the room when she had died, took us in to see her. Other than that there is very little I remember about it. I don't think we were allowed to go to the funeral when my mother died – somebody else must have looked after us or something.

leaving the district

There was only two other brothers and another sister living down there at the finish. The others had all gone. There was no money to keep everyone so Grace and I went off to Hokitika and we both got work at the Seaview Hospital. Then we went from there to the Franz Josef Glacier and worked at the hotel down there. At that time five shillings a week was as much as you were getting. If you got two pounds you were on a very high wage.

Death at Okuru

Mrs Eggeling first complained about a pain in her side in the Tuesday, and had to go to bed on Wednesday and had a very bad night. Nurse Baker (happily in the neighbourhood) was sent for on Thursday and after examining the patient reported the case serious. Mr Wild was asked to despatch a steamer, but as no reply was received, Mr Geo. Perry was appealed to with the result that a steamer was to be despatched on Friday night sea permitting. Wild or Jolly's price, I hear was to be £75 for the trip. Only fancy making a lever of the urgent aid to demand £75. Through Mr Perry's efforts two doctors made a record trip to Okuru … Everybody tried to assist the Nolan bros., in arranging the relay of horses from the Waiho to the Haast, where Mr D. Nolan with three horses in a gig met the doctors and covered the ten miles along the beach to Okuru in one hour 5 minutes including the crossing of the Okuru and Turnbull rivers, arriving at Eggeling's home at 3pm on the Sunday.

The Doctors rested an hour and the operation was successfully performed by 5.30 o'clock, Sister Baker having arranged everything in advance. Sister Baker's professional services were recognised by the residents of Okuru with a purse of sovereigns and a testimonial. Much sympathy expressed by the whole of the district to Mr Eggeling and family, to him, in losing a help mate and to the children for the loss of a loving and kind mother.

Doctors Baird & Buchanan
One cannot but admire, or let pass unnoticed the brilliant achievement of Drs Baird and Buchanan in their recent race from Hokitika to Okuru … Over 200 miles in 34 hours with conditions and obstacles such as these men encountered is nothing short of a record. Considering that these men had not ridden a horse for years and seeing that the latter part of the journey (over 100 miles) had to be traversed on horseback speaks well of their determination and indefatigable energy … The assistance given to the doctors by the settlers en route should not pass unnoticed. Horses and guides were available at every stage, clearly demonstrating the fellow feeling and brotherly love for which Westlanders are characteristic.

Hokitika Guardian and Evening Star 16 May 1921

Charlie and Dick were still farming when we left. Dick got married and things evidently didn't go right there. They parted and she went away. Charlie, he married Betty Buchanan. Betty was a lot younger than Charlie but they were very happy. They done everything together, they were a great couple. When they were married they spent their honeymoon with me. They never had a car and they had nowhere much to go, so they came and spent two nights with us at Souters Creek [near Ngahere] on their honeymoon.

Charlie and Dick were very similar in lots of ways. Dick was very, very good to Betty and Charlie. When they were out doing

things or wanted to go anywhere, he'd look after the children. He also used to make pickles and jams and all sorts of things like that. Betty has always been an outdoor girl. She loved outside on the farm and she'd rather be outside than in doing housework. She was lucky that she had him there to help her.

After [Seaview Hospital], well we worked in hotels and round about like that. Worked down at the Franz Josef for a long time, Fox Glacier, went down to Stewart Island and worked down there for a while. We travelled round together for years.

Arthur's sister worked at the Franz Josef where I had been working and we became very friendly. I came up and stayed at her place for a week in the holidays and that was where I met him. Our friendship developed and we got married. After we got married we went out past Nelson Creek to a little place called Souters Creek. We had no neighbours there or anything. We had three boys out there and it was when the oldest one was ready for school we shifted into Ngahere [Grey Valley], and I've been at Ngahere ever since.

We didn't sort of like leaving down there but at the same time there was nothing to keep us. We felt that we had to get out if we wanted to do anything for ourselves. Well, you've got to get out and earn your own money. There wasn't enough to keep the lot of us.

It's not really the same. Betty's the only one there now, and there is sort of nothing else to go back for. I think it was [a good place to grow up in]. I don't think it done any of us any harm. I think the lack of education meant a terrible lot. When you come away out of it you are so innocent, it takes you a while to get accepted by some. You haven't got the confidence which you have if you are working and mixing with people and if you have a good education.

Ruby (left) with her sister Grace.
Courtesy of Ann Mackey

Charlie Eggeling with a catch of whitebait.
From The New Zealanders in Colour by Kenneth and Jean Bigwood

*Bridget Cron
(née Cox)
1843–1901.*
Courtesy of Eunice
Cron

*Adam Cron
1836–1904.*
Courtesy of Cliff Cron

Ancestors of Allan Cron

Adam CRON
Born: c. 1836 in Scotland
Married: 1867 in Hokitika, Westland
Died: August 1904 in Hokit ka, Westland
Arrived Jackson Bay: 19 January 1875

Michael John CRON
Born: c. 1872 in Kaniere, Westland
Married: 1899 in Haast, Westland
Died: March 1953 in Hokitika, Westland

Bridget COX
Born: c. 1843 in Ireland
Died: October 1901 in Haast, Westland
Arrived Jackson Bay: 19 January 1875

Allan Andrew CRON
Born: 1912 in Haast, Westland

Andrew NOLAN
Born: c. 1842 in Ireland
Married: 1871 in Stafford, Westland
Died: September 1914 in Hokitika, Westland
Arrived Jackson Bay: 12 April 1875

Norah NOLAN
Born: 1879 in Jackson Bay, Westland
Died: 1962 in Haast, Westland

Mary SPILLANE
Born: c. 1849 in Ireland
Died: April 1920 in Hokitika, Westland
Arrived Jackson Bay: 12 April 1875

Chapter 5

'He ran a clinic on the back verandah and pulled 96 teeth'

Allan Cron

Allan was born in 1912 at Haast, the fourth child of John Cron and Norah (née Nolan). Educated mostly in Christchurch, he became interested in flying and made his first flight at Christchurch in 1930. His link to South Westland and his friendship with Bert Mercer were instrumental in starting an air service to Haast. With the outbreak of World War Two, Allan was needed on the family farm near Haast River and his flying days ended. Known to his friends as 'Old Crikey', Allan had a fantastic sense of humour and even though he was not well when we recorded this interview, we had a lot of laughs. He was married three times and has three daughters and a son who still farms at Haast. Allan passed away in July 1996.

the war news

My mother used to run the post office at Haast. I can remember when the First World War stopped because my mother called my father and the various men about and said, 'Come and have a drink – the war's over!' They all had a drink and everything was all right, and then a few days after they found that it was only a false alarm. I hadn't a clue what a false alarm was. I knew what an alarm clock was but what a false alarm was, I had not a clue! It was about three weeks before the war came to a halt and the boys started to wander home.

My mother took the war news over the phone, every night. I think she might have pinned a notice up. Things used to get muddled up. It was supposed to be British bore brunt, but it came over as British boar burnt. Old man Condon heard it [Allan begins imitating someone with a slight stutter]: 'By joves, those Germans are awful fellows, they are even burning the pigs now.' There was no radio and everything came by phone, and of course the people who were receiving it could make mistakes.

Allan Cron when he was sixty-five.
Courtesy of Eunice Cron

Allan Cron with his family, c. 1920. Back (left to right): Florrie, Jack, Ivy. Front: Norah (née Nolan), Allan, John and Myrtle.

Courtesy of Eunice Cron

a visiting dentist

My father received a letter from a man in Christchurch. He wanted some information. There was a party of them were going to walk through the Haast Pass and up the coast. He was a dental surgeon and my sister Ivy had four wisdom teeth that needed extracting. She said to my father, 'When you reply ask him to bring a set of forceps and some local anaesthetic.' Anyway, these people came eventually and the man's name was Wilfred Ward. He'd brought the forceps and oodles of local anaethestic. He said to my father, 'I'd be prepared to stop here today and do any dental work that people want done if you take me through to the Maitai [Mahitahi] on horseback so that I can catch up with my friends.' Father was quite agreeable to that. So Mother rang around everyone and, oh yes, a lot of them wanted teeth done. Anyway to make a long story short, he ran a clinic on the back verandah and pulled ninety-six teeth. They came from far and near!

broken ankles and horses

I was up Gap Creek and it was very rough. I was coming out and I went over on my ankle. The pain was something incredible. The creek was right there, of course, so I went and put the foot in it. I thought that should ease it down, but it didn't. So I wandered out to the track. I thought, well, I will have to carry on walking because it might be six months before anyone comes along. I would go so far, and the boot would be absolutely tight and painful so I would loosen it a bit and put it in a creek and then carry on again. Eventually I got to down to my father's place. I was in bed with it for quite a while but I hadn't a clue that it was broken. I found out it was broken after I came up here to Blenheim [50 years later]. I had to have an X-ray for something else and they said, 'You've had it broken at one time.' I said, 'Have I?' 'Yes!' and I said, 'Oh, I didn't know. I thought it was only sprained.' 'No no, it was broken.'

My father and Uncle Ted were going up to do some mustering up the Landsborough. My uncle had a yellow dog – he had several dogs, but this one was a yellow one – and it took after a deer. Ted was riding along. The road was only just wide enough for a horse to stand on, and this dog comes bursting out of the bush and the horse jumped sideways into space. It went down about sixty feet down onto the boulders. My father made my uncle as comfortable as he could on the riverbed and turned tail and went down to get some men to carry him on a stretcher down to Haast. Oh, it would have been about twenty miles. He had a lot of injuries. He lived but he never walked properly again. I think that was the cause of his cancer really.

We were going to do some mustering up the Landsborough. I'd forded the Haast River on my horse and we had a bit of a scramble getting ashore. There was a little bit of swampy ground and she staggered a bit, and I thought she was just staggering, and then down she went. She was lying on my leg, but underneath the ground was soft and I pulled myself out. I took the bridle and saddle off. I could see she was dead. I was able to pick a ford in the Haast and got onto the road. My son brought

Adventurous canoe voyage	An adventurous voyage in a log canoe down the Haast, one of the principal rivers on the West Coast, was undertaken by a young South Westland man, Mr. Alan [sic] Cron, of the Haast Settlement. It was the first trip of its kind for many years … Mr. Cron, who was supervising work on the landing ground on Landsborough Flats, far up the Haast River, found it necessary to get down to a homestead near the coast. There had been such bad weather that he felt it unlikely that any aeroplane would make the trip up the gorge. No horse was available, so he set sail in the early morning in a log canoe which he had hollowed out of a huge log some months ago. He attached an outrigger to the canoe to secure greater stability and set out on the long journey home. Mr. Cron's journey is typical of the hardihood and resource of the men who live in these isolated areas in the far south, where roads are not yet built and rivers, instead of being crossed by bridges, are crossed in boats and on horseback.

Weekly News 7 June 1939

along a vehicle and I was able to drive myself home. So I said, that's it – no more mustering for me. I never went mustering again.

characters in the district

Allan Cron at fifty.
Courtesy of
Eunice Cron

I heard of Jimmy Stout – he was gone before my time. Mrs McPherson and Jimmy Stout had half shares in a boat and they quarrelled. She asked this old German bloke to blow it up and he put a charge of gelignite in the bow and blew the bow off. Old Stout come down and found the boat and was really cross. The boat was floating but you couldn't get in to row it, so he got in the stern and the bow went up of course and he rowed it up the river that way. Slow but sure. Then one of her daughters, I think it was Jess, got a cross-cut saw and sawed it in half. He couldn't do anything about that!

Jimmy Stout had an orchard and he sold fruit, up the Turnbull River, not far up. This is the best story I heard about him. The authorities had a man to be hung in Hokitika. They asked for anyone who was interested to put in a tender. Old Jimmy, he put in a price of thirty shillings. He would have had to go from Okuru to Hokitika on horseback, which would take about a fortnight and a fortnight back, and he was gonna get thirty bob. Anyway, there was a bloke in Hokitika beat him – he put in a quote of a pound. Jimmy was done out of his thirty shillings.

The McPhersons? I remember the two eldest boys. Donald, the younger one – he went to the First World War and was telling me that a bottle of rum saved his life. He and his mate, a chap Billy Grey, they'd made a bed under a wagon. Donald was in the artillery you see. They went away to get a bottle of rum, and while they were away the Germans started shelling and the shells were coming thick and fast. Eventually, when it eased off, they went back to the wagon and there was only a big hole in the ground.

Ann [Mackey]'s grandfather came from Germany and he handled the English language, you know, a bit roughly. He was foreman on the track. It was dynamite then, before gelignite come in. Dynamite would get hard and you would have to warm it up. You could buy a warmer, a little pan thing with a jacket around it that you put the hot water in.

Memories of Myrtle & Ivy Cron

Allan's siblings are well remembered in the Haast district, particularly two of his sisters:

Myrtle and Ivy, I knew them quite well. They were just ladies that were more or less pioneers, like a lot of us. They were hard and, you know, pretty tough. Myrtle used to go out and shoot and skin deer and all sorts like that, castrate her own calves, brand the stock – she was quite a lady, a real lady, you know. A land lady. Ivy did the ferry after her father got too old to do it, rowing the boat across the Haast River and ferrying people for quite some years.

Well, I think people just sort of did what they had to do. If you had to do it, you did it. You know, I think those ladies were every bit as good as any man – probably better than a lot. If something had to be done and it was for them to do it, they did it and that was about all there was to it.
Recollections of Ted Buchanan, 1996

Myrtle Cron at the West Coast Airways Office at Haast. Courtesy of Paul Beauchamp Legg

Myrtle Cron? Oh yes, she was a character. She could swear like a man, act like a man, shoot like a man. She was annoyed with one of the whitebaiters in the Haast River one night so she shot holes through his whitebait net. Ivy mostly did the ferry. You used to have to fire three shots if you wanted the ferry. Then they'd come and get you, if they heard you.
Recollections of Henry Buchanan, 1995

Anyway, they couldn't be bothered with that. What they'd do, they'd light a fire on the ground, and when things were well and truly hotted up they'd rake the fire away and put the dynamite on the hot earth. Well anyway, it would only soften one side, you'd have to come round and turn it. So old August put it there and softened one side, and he went and turned it, and he was just going away and bang she went. He was a very mean old fella and [Allan breaks into song, complete with German accent]:

> *I was just going away*
> *When the whole thing let fly*
> *Rackwood and matches went up towards the sky*
> *I was kinda sort of sorry*
> *That I had to run away*
> *For I woulda got a decent passage up*
> *And I wouldna had to pay!*

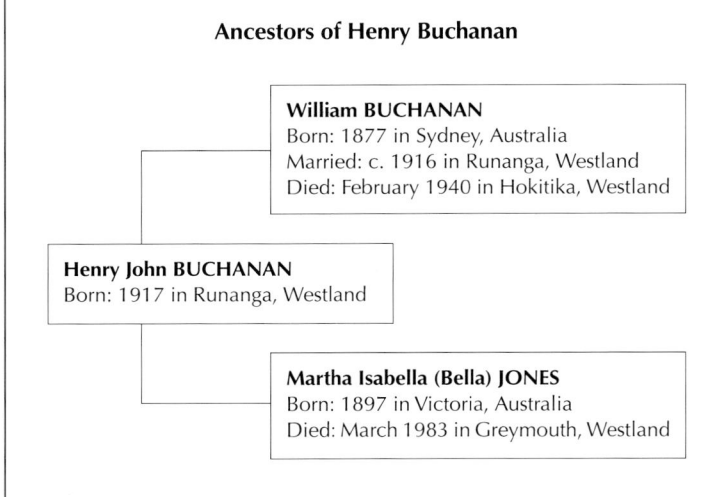

Ancestors of Henry Buchanan

William BUCHANAN
Born: 1877 in Sydney, Australia
Married: c. 1916 in Runanga, Westland
Died: February 1940 in Hokitika, Westland

Henry John BUCHANAN
Born: 1917 in Runanga, Westland

Martha Isabella (Bella) JONES
Born: 1897 in Victoria, Australia
Died: March 1983 in Greymouth, Westland

Henry Buchanan (centre) with his parents, William and Bella, and younger brother, Bill. Courtesy of Henry Buchanan

Chapter 6

'I've been a bushman most of my life'

Henry Buchanan

Henry was the eldest child of William Buchanan and Bella (née Jones), and was born at Rununga (near Greymouth) where his father was working as a coalminer. Younger siblings (Bill, Betty, Myra, Bruce and Ted), were born at Ross and Ikamatua. The family moved several times following work before finally shifting to Okuru in the early 1930s. Henry lived in the Haast district for most of his life and spent his final years living at Jackson Bay. He was a well-known raconteur and had a wide circle of friends both young and old. He was married twice and had a large family. Henry passed away in 1997.

moving to Haast

From Ikamatua we shifted down to here, down to Okuru. We shifted all our cows, horses, cattle, children – the whole lot. It was a real Noah's Ark experience. We travelled down on the *Gael*. It was about 1930, I think, I was fourteen anyhow. I had just left school. Dad bought bush here. He was still working for Wallis and they came down and took up bush and bought the farm, and he decided to shift down here.

Dad took up a claim on the north Haast Beach, a gold claim. We worked there for quite a long while, would have been about three years, I think.

Henry Buchanan at Jackson Bay, 1996.
Julia Bradshaw

We were blacksanding, shovelling black sand onto the plush mats and streaming it off with water. You had to carry water up, two buckets at a time. I spent a lot of my young life doing that, two buckets of water heading up the beach. Daylight till dark. He got quite a lot of gold out of it; it put us on our feet here. If it wasn't for the gold, I don't know what we would have done.

He had this farm up the Turnbull and then he took up the Jackson run. We ran quite a few cattle up there. My brother mostly took on the farming when Dad died. Then we built a sawmill over the North Okuru. We cut all the timber for the early bridge-building here. The road construction company were building the bridges, and we were cutting the timber and getting the piles and that sort of work. It wasn't very big, a small show driven by a tractor. It did about a thousand feet a day, that was about all we'd manage, I think.

family life

It was mostly my job to look after the garden. Mine and Mum's as a rule. She and I used to do all the ploughing. We used to put in about an acre of potatoes, that was the main thing and we used to plough that, but the other garden was only about ten metres square. We mostly grew cabbages, lettuces, peas and beans. Wood pigeons, we ate quite a good mound of those. We had a good tree just outside the house.

William Buchanan outside his hut on Okuru River, c. 1940s. Courtesy of Henry Buchanan

When the miro berries were out, we'd knock them over and have a big roast up. We mostly stewed them, they made beautiful stew. And pies, Mum used to put a pie crust on and they were absolutely lovely to eat. Specially with the miro – miro berries gave them a special taste.

Occasionally we'd have beef but not very often because there were no freezers in those days. You couldn't kill a beast and say you'd put half away in the freezer because you didn't have one. Once more people came you starting killing a beast and sharing it all around. It was quite good then.

We always had loads of cream and butter. We milked cows and made butter. Harkers tearooms in Greymouth used to buy all our butter because it was good for making pastry with. They used to buy all we could make. We used to make it for ourselves and keep it salted down for the winter, but it used to get real rancid. Oh, it was awful stuff! I often wondered how you could eat it – we did though. It was mostly pretty basic what we lived on.

Okuru was *the* settlement in those days. A road went as far as Haast – it was a dray track not a road, there was a road to Nolans', a road to our place, to Harris's. You could ride down to Jackson Bay. You had to ford all the rivers an' all that. You had to work the tide and go when the tide was low. The rivers were always dangerous.

It was a marvellous thing [when Bert Mercer started flying]. We all went out and built an airstrip at Mussel Point. We had grubbers and shovels and barrows and all sorts of things. It was a good thing for the district. You could always get an emergency plane in if anyone was sick.

Before that you had to carry them out by stretcher through to Paringa.

scrub clearing

I've been a bushman most of my life, though I got around to being a fisherman, a deer culler and all sorts of things. I cut bush down the Cascade for Nolans, on contract. I was down at Doolans, for a couple of years I suppose. I was only a young guy then, only about sixteen or seventeen.

There were three or four gangs doing the same thing. We chopped out all Doolans' paddock and we did some further up Burgesses, we cleared a lot there. It was very hard work. There was Noel Saxton with us and I forget the others. We had a hut there, an iron hut. We had no bath or showers or toilets.

The work involved clearing all these niggerhead ferns [prickly shield fern, *polystichum vestitum*], hearting them. You've got to get them right down to the heart or they'll grow again. It was back-breaking work. You'd crawl home at night and you wouldn't even be bothered with any tea. You'd get straight to bed. You were too had-it to do anything. We used to eat well, though. I remember Kelly Wilson was down there with me one time and we had a twelve-inch camp oven full of potatoes, and he and I ate the lot! We'd kill a sheep a week, I think.

We were paid by W.D. Nolan. We earned £3 10s. I think it was, an acre to completely clear it, fell it all. Then they'd burn it and sow it with grass seed and away it would go. It was farmland then. There was a government subsidy on it. They paid so much and he paid so much, and that's the way it worked. We'd be in there a couple of months – three months sometimes.

working on the road

When I first started on the road, it only went as far as Makarora. I stayed on there until it was up to Fantail Falls. I was working for old Ben Drake, an old fella from Hawea. I was driving horses and drays for him and he was building the road. Then this bulldozer came up the river. It was the first one I ever saw in my life. Oh gawd, didn't it make a mess in a short time! We couldn't believe what it could do. It was such a turnaround from picks and shovels. There was a road there in no time. We were more or less obsolete.

I worked on the Haast Road for quite a while. Then I came to this side and I started carting shingle and clearing bush. I cleared all the bush from Waiatoto to Okuru. We had a contract to do it. There was myself, Noel Saxton, Squinny McMahon and Arthur Carter we were the gang that worked on the road. We had a cross-cut saw, axes, hammer and wedges, a couple of jacks to jack the logs off the side with. That was it. Between Carters [Hannahs Clearing] and Waiatoto took us about twelve months, I think. We had to clear it thirty feet wide and shift all the big logs

Roadworks at Makarora, during the 1930s.
Thelma Kent Collection, Alexander Turnbull Library/Te Puna Mātauranga o Aotearoa, F- 9205-1/2

off, and that took quite a while. Dave Weir and the Green brothers – they imported a big steam winch and they winched it down the roadway, and then put blocks off the side and pulled them [stumps] off the road. Then the lorries came along with the shingle and filled it all in.

Jim Dennehy came in with his trucks. He had the Ford surgery up there. That's where I cut my teeth on Fords. I never want to see another one in my life. Every time you went out in them they broke down. 'I'll just take her back to the surgery,' old Jim Dennehy would say. He'd be working there on the trucks. It was a full-time job. He had four trucks, I think, and he was a full-time mechanic on them.

Oh good money, yes. I got all the telephone poles too, did all that on contract to the Works. We used to go into the bush about eight in the morning and by half-past ten we'd be home. We'd got all the money we were allowed to earn. Once you'd earned so much, you never went on with it, because if you did, you'd be cut next time, your price would be down. So you had to work as much as you were allowed to make and then holiday the rest of the day. On the road-clearing it was so much a chain, and on the telephone poles they used to pay us per pole. But they'd only let you make a maximum of £8 a day. If you made any more, your next contract would be cut. We used to be boating around the river, fishing and doing all sorts of things.

crays at Jackson Bay

They had a post office here in the bay. Mike Lee and Ned Early were the post people. Messages were sent out by morse code. Mike Lee used to catch crayfish off the wharf here with ring pots. He had a system rigged up – he hooked his car onto the pot and pulled it up with the car, you see. So he never had to put any strength into it. He said it was brains against brawn. Mike caught a lot of crayfish one time and sent them up to a do we had in Haast. But he didn't tell them that he'd murdered all these kittens. The cat had kittens so he murdered all the kittens and caught the crayfish with the dead kittens. The women were spewing up there when he told them he'd caught them with dead kittens.

whitebaiting

It was about 1950 that I first started fishing. National Mortgage Company from Dunedin sent boats around here because they were trawling crayfish. They had a freezer and they set it up on the wharf out here. They sent a great big trawler round which would collect all the fish, and all the other trawlers just stayed here and fished into this freezer. Eventually they left and I bought the freezer from them. That started me into the whitebait then, and that's how I got into big trouble because I was in direct opposition with the Nolans.

Things in the old whitebait days, you know, they were pretty hairy. Old Nolan – he was ruling like a Czar, and he'd tell you where you could fish and where you could go. He told me I could fish the Okuru River one time. He had a boy on every river – he had five boys, you see, and if he had a boy on the river you weren't allowed to fish there, otherwise he wouldn't take your fish. He told me one time, 'You can fish the Okuru this year.' His boy had been fishing it and he hadn't been doing any good so he shifted him off the Okuru. We had the Turnbull because our whole family were there. He said I could fish the Okuru, so I fished it and I made about £600, I think it was – it was a big amount of money anyway. He didn't want to pay me, it was too much money for a boy. I said, 'I earned it Mr Nolan; I want it.' Eventually he said, 'Oh well, I'll pay it, but we catered for you.' And I said, 'Well, anything you gave me you can take out of it.' I think he took out £66, something like that, and I said to him that I could have lived at the Chateau Tongariro for less. That was the start of the whitebait wars then.

I had this freezer, you see, and I thought I'll get into this whitebait too. So we put our own whitebait in our freezer for a start and then I started buying as well, on the side. Then we really got into wars then. I started flying it out. Before I even got the freezer, I flew whitebait out. I flew it out with [Arthur] Bradshaw, flew it over to Cromwell. He had a Puss Moth, a little wee bloody thing. He used to fly down the Waiatoto and we'd put the tins along the beach so he could count how many tins of whitebait we had. Then he'd go up and wait for us at Mussel Point and we'd have to pack them up on the packhorse. It'd take a couple of hours.

When we were fishing for Nolan we were getting thruppence a pound. When we started with Bradshaw he was giving us a shilling a pound. We were way ahead, we thought. Then when I started on my own, when I got the freezer, I was paying thirty shillings a tin. I used to fly it all out to Christchurch with West Coast Airways.

I was buying from all the fishermen round here – they were mostly locals. Of course, I was paying them a lot more than they'd get at the factory. Not long after that, a couple of years after I think, Nolans started doing the same thing. They started flying it too, then we had big rows on airspace. There'd be all sorts of rows when the Nolans would be up there with bait and I'd be there and we'd both want to get our bait on the plane, and of course we didn't always get it on. The Nolans and the Crons were related and Myrtle Cron was the agent for West Coast Airways. Gawd, we had some bloody donnybrooks over getting fish on!

Problems with the weather? A lot of it I'd take down and tip in the river. You'd take it out of the freezer so many times, and you'd take it out to the airport and you'd sit there and wait all day, and by the time you brought it back and did that two or three times the bait was rotten. You'd get word to say that the plane had left, but then it would get down half-way and go back again. There's a big bottleneck at Okarito, all that low swampland. It used to fog very heavily and they'd get down that far and they'd be stopped – couldn't get any further.

deer shooting

I learnt about deer shooting mostly from the Harrises. George and Joe Harris used to own the Okuru run. They used to take me up there when I was a lad and tell me all sorts of stories. Got me to shoot a few deer. That's where I first started shooting. Bernie Cowan and I, we knocked around a lot in the early days, shooting. Every weekend I was up there, you know – if it was a good weekend I'd be away.

Henry with his brothers; Ted is on the left and Bruce on the right, c. 1976.
Courtesy of Neville Peat

I started doing it full time in about 1955–1960. We built a factory at Greymouth and we did venison in that right through to about 1978–80, around there. We started buying. We were paying a shilling a pound, I think, for venison. Which was quite good money for the amount that were about, they were pretty plentiful. And then we used to fly them out to Greymouth, process them there. Sent our first load to USA, but they were very finicky. Then we got into the German market, and we started sending them there after that – they were a lot less particular.

'Course the skins were valuable those times too. We used to get about ten shillings a skin, which was big money in those days. We used to go up the Haast a lot at night, in the landrover. We'd generally get a dozen or fifteen, something like that.

We started off with a freezer at the aerodrome at Greymouth and then we took over a building up in Williams Street and turned it into a factory. We started processing in there and ran [cray]fish as well but then we had to separate them because the MAF wouldn't let us do the venison and the fish in one factory. So we built another one. In the finish it was colossal, really. We had agents everywhere and chillers. We used to go around with trucks and empty them. It was quite an industry in the finish. We probably had 100–150 shooters.

Then other firms started. Westland Frozen Products, they started exporting venison and that sort of cut us back. I had three aeroplanes at that time and we mostly flew all the venison out to the factory, which gave us a bit of a head start on the others. Graham Stewart's, they came in with helicopters and God knows what. Multi-million dollar outfit. They eventually put us out of business. I never ever thought the deer would be silly enough to stand there and let the helicopter shoot them or I'd have had one years ago. When I bought the Apache I should have bought a helicopter, I would have been right amongst it then.

fishing

It must have been about 1950 we started crayfishing. It was when the crayfish were thick here and they sent the boats around from Dunedin. It was mostly day trips when we first started because there was plenty of them there. You'd only have to go to the head, only a few hundred yards out. We had no winch on the boat – we used to lift the whole lot up by hand. What a back-breaking outfit; you've no idea what it was like! Bruce, my brother, and Phil Pendergast were doing the fishing in the wee boat [*Cascade*] for a kickoff and I was doing the distributing side of it. I would look after the crayfish and keep the freezer going. Take it to the planes and all that sort of thing. You had to have someone there to do it. Then we took the boat to Greymouth – I think Bruce took it up actually – and got the winches put on. We were away then, home and hosed. It was fun then.

Then we decided to get a bigger boat so we built the *Bonita*. We used to go down for a two-month trip. It had a ten-ton hold and we'd fill it with tails and then come home again. There was only three of us on the boat. We'd mostly fly the tails out from here to Greymouth, to our factory where we used to pack them.

We had some big storms in there. Oh yeah, plenty of hair-raising experiences. One time we went into Bligh Sound and the weather came away at night. It was just before daylight actually, and I could feel the boat wasn't right. I could feel it bumping and I thought, hey that's the bottom! So I away up out of bed and up the stairs, I had the motor going as I was coming up. I was yelling, 'Hey, you jokers – get up and get those anchors up!' We'd set three anchors but the sound bottom there is very loose, you know it's just mud, no holding at all. So we got up by the short shirt-tails and got the anchors up. We steamed up and down all day, just up and down the reach because it was blowing so hard. It blew a cast-iron pot off the foredeck right down to the aft of the boat. A cast-iron pot! I remember a chap going to get some coal. We were carrying some coal up the front of the boat in bags, three or four bags tied around the mast. He dived the shovel into the bag, pulled it out of the bag and whoosh like that, there wasn't one bit of coal left on the shovel! Oh gawd, blow! You've never seen anything like it. The *Crusader* was in there and it was only a little thing. The damn mast was just about right on the water at times, blowing right over. We had to steam up and down there. Luckily it broke just before dark and it came out a beautiful night. I was frightened it was going to go on into the night. I don't know how we would have got on. We wouldn't have been able to see where we were going. At times you couldn't see with the water rising off the sound – it was picking the water up in sheets. Screaming wind, just screaming.

Why did I stop fishing? Because I got too old! Got rheumatics in my hands and arthritis was setting in and I thought, hey I'd better get out of this, or I mightn't be around much longer. I was getting crook knees and that.

first car

The first car was here – oh, when would that be – in the 1950s, I suppose. There wasn't even a road out or anything, you couldn't get out anywhere. Old Dinny Nolan bought an old Model A and he used to drive from here to Haast and around the Okuru. The roads were pretty rough, they were only really dray tracks. He ran off the road going up the Okuru there once. I said, 'What happened, Mr Nolan?' 'I don't know,' he said. 'She shied.' He reckoned the car had shied!

Dick and Charlie [Eggeling] had a Ford, an old thing. Old Charlie and Dick, they were pretty late learning to drive. They were probably in their fifties when they got this truck. They used to back into pits and Charlie would be walking alongside and Dick would be there at the wheel, looking straight ahead. Charlie would be telling him which way to turn the wheel, and Charlie would tell him the wrong way and then they'd have an argument. We used to go round there and watch them doing it. Laugh! It was hilarious watching them backing into a pit.

coming and going

I was up in Greymouth for quite a while. I always liked down here though. I'd be back and forth. Then I decided to get out altogether, the weather drove me out, and I went mussel farming near Blenheim, about 1980. It was too blooming windy. It was screaming wind one way or the other, because you are right in Cook Strait. You get the full brunt of it. Lovely weather – but the wind, it would drive you nuts.

I came back down here – I got sick of the mussels. You couldn't sell the damn things at one part of it, you know. It was a heart–breaking outfit. I came down whitebaiting, and I thought to hell with them, I'm not going back. So I bought a house down here and stayed here.

It would be for better, for sure. It would have to be. You don't get anyone dying now because they can't get out to a doctor. If you want to go anywhere now, you hop in your car and away you go. Before you had to saddle up a horse and ride 300 miles and then get into a car and go somewhere else. It would take you a month to get there. No, life's a lot better. I think the aircraft was the real turning point for the district. And of course the road going through the Haast was a big thing too.

Andrew Nolan. Courtesy *of Bill Nolan*

Ancestors of Des Nolan

Andrew NOLAN
Born: c. 1842 in Ireland
Married: 1871 in Stafford, Westland
Died: September 1914 in Hokitika, Westland
Arrived Jackson Bay: 12 April 1875

William Denis (Din) NOLAN
Born: 1877 in Jackson Bay, Westland
Married: 1913 in Hokitika, Westland
Died: November 1959 in Hokitika, Westland

Mary SPILLANE
Born: c. 1849 in Ireland
Died: April 1920 in Hokitika, Westland
Arrived Jackson Bay: 12 April 1875

Desmond (Des) Joseph NOLAN
Born: 1920 in Hokitika, Westland

Mary RITCHIE
Born: 1884 in Jacobs River, Westland
Died: 1948 in Hokitika, Westland

Chapter 7

'I rode my first bucking horse when I was about eight'

Des Nolan

Des was born in Hokitika in 1920 and was the second-youngest of the five sons of Din (Denis) Nolan and Mary (née Ritchie). The family lived at Okuru where Din Nolan's parents had been farming since 1885. In 1953 Des married Eileen Maunsell, a nurse at the hospital in Hokitika, and the couple had three children. Eileen passed away in 1981 and Des lived in retirement on the land where he had spent nearly all his life. In the 2001 New Years Honours list, Des was made a Member of the New Zealand Order of Merit (MNZM) for services to aviation in South Westland. He passed away in April 2001.

My grandfather, he got caught up in this bloomin' scheme of Jackson Bay. It was supposed to be the land of milk and honey,

Des Nolan at Okuru, 1999.
Julia Bradshaw

gold on the beaches and all that. He went down there in the rush to Jackson Bay. It went on for a few years but it proved to be a fiasco and a lot of the people went back out again on the boat, that'd be the only way to go. Grandad Nolan, like some of the other early pioneers, came over here to Okuru, looking for farmland, you see. They came up the Okuru River here and took land up.

farming

My dad, he and his brother Paddy, they were farming together. Me dad bought the Cascade Valley from a chap Fraser a long time ago. There was the Arawhata River, Okuru and Copper Creek runs. Us boys actually bought Uncle Paddy out when he left. That'd be about 1942, something like that. About the time of the war. We carried on farming all those places for quite a number of years. There was five of us [brothers] here, but Bill was away at the war for three years and Eddie left and went to Ranfurly. Eventually Bill got a farm in Leeston, so there were the three of us brothers – Robbie, Kevin and I – here. Anyway, we decided to split the farm up into three blocks. That was quite a big job. We farmed on our own account from then on.

We didn't have a lot of machinery as far as farming went. There was no tractors – it was all horse. There was a steam engine up here that ran the sawmill. We had our own sawmill, you see. It was an old Marshall steam engine. It had been used for flax milling. It was actually brought down from up at the Waita [River], which is about nine or ten miles north of Haast. They brought it down with a great team of horses – I think there was at least sixteen horses. They gathered horses from around the district.

Des Nolan (left) and his brother Kevin on Christmas Day, 1927.

Courtesy of Bill Nolan

The sawmill operated as required. If we wanted timber we would just knock off and do some milling. There again the logs were brought in with horses, a team of horses. It was all horses. They got quite a good price at sales, probably about £40 which was more than cattle brought, at that time. They used to breed at least twenty a year down at Cascade for a time. Once the tractors came in, the price of horses just dropped, so it wasn't bothered with any more.

Of course there was a lot of breaking in done in those days. It was another thing that took a lot of time and a certain amount of skill and knowledge. I rode my first bucking horse when I was about eight. I've been off and on them ever since.

Des Nolan (at left) with his parents and brothers.
Courtesy of Bill Nolan

getting the cattle
to market

We used to take the cattle up to Copper Creek, we had a fifty-acre holding paddock there. They'd spell there for two or three days prior to going on the track over the Paringa Saddle. The first day was the biggest day – it was twenty miles actually. Eight miles up to the Iron Hut and twelve miles from there to Blue River. It was a mighty big day, twenty miles and a hill to climb as well. It was all uphill to the Iron Hut. Sometimes we'd bring along a bit of drink and sometimes we wouldn't be very well the next morning! At Blue River – it was more of a yard than a paddock – they used to be held in there. The next day was only about eleven miles out to

Paringa. We'd spell there in a paddock of Condon's. The next day was to Jacobs River which was another fairly big day. Then it wasn't such a big day to Karangarua, to Scotts' place, where we used a paddock. We'd give them a day's spell there.

We'd take through mobs of up to 200 sometimes. Sometimes some of the neighbouring farmers would join in the drive. Likes of the Harrises on several occasions and Donald McPherson, he'd come too. It wasn't a bad idea to go through together. They'd be at least half a dozen [men] over the Paringa Saddle, that was the problem part you might

The Haast-Paringa cattle track. The track followed a route used by Maori for hundreds of years.

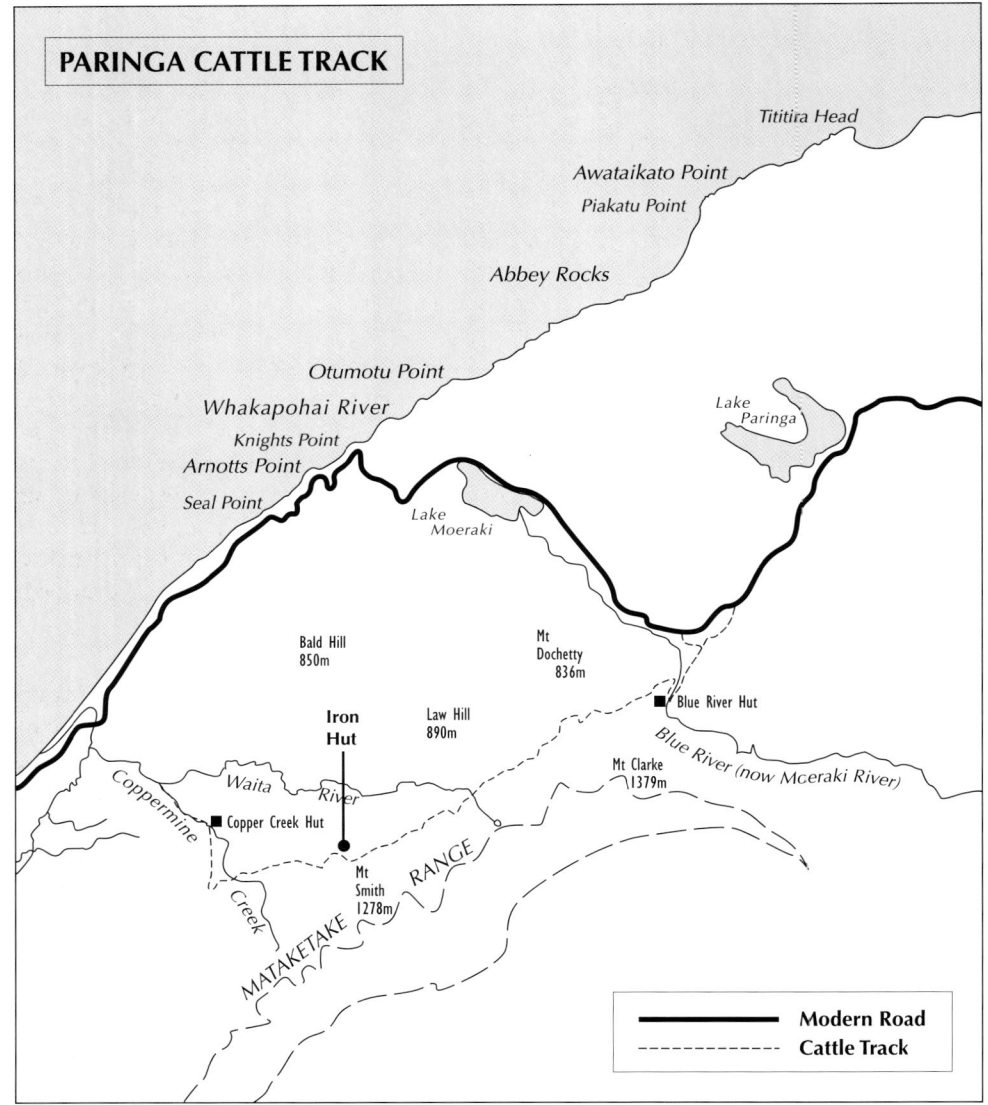

PARINGA CATTLE TRACK

Tititira Head

Awataikato Point

Piakatu Point

Abbey Rocks

Otumotu Point

Whakapohai River

Knights Point

Arnotts Point

Seal Point

Lake Paringa

Lake Moeraki

Bald Hill
850m

Mt Dochetty
836m

Blue River Hut

Iron Hut

Law Hill
890m

Blue River (now Mceraki River)

Mt Clarke
1379m

Coppermine

Waita River

■ Copper Creek Hut

Mt Smith
1278m

MATAKETAKE RANGE

Creek

——————— **Modern Road**

- - - - - - - - - **Cattle Track**

say. A sidling road and slips and narrow tracks and creeks. You know, it was a bit of a hill-billy thing in a way. The roadman always used to keep it reasonably passable. Mostly two or three men would take them on the rest of the journey to Whataroa, because there was big wide roads and not a lot of problems at that end.

Occasionally [we'd lose cattle]. That first day over Paringa Saddle there was the odd one lost, but not a lot. They'd generally be recovered. They'd get up or be got up, and they'd end up back down at Cattle Creek with the cattle there. The roadmen were characters in their own right. They were very hospitable people. They didn't have much but they would share with the traveller what they did have. They were very generous people like that.

drownings

There were some close shaves with people getting drowned. I suppose I had one real close one myself, one time. In the Haast. It was after rain and there was a fresh in the river. My brother Bill and I were going up to muster at Copper Creek. He would have been first in the river but he had to go back and pick a dog up. I passed him and I was on an excitable little horse – he wasn't much good in the water really. It was a downstream ford which is awkward in so far as if you decide to opt out of it, well then you've got the current against you trying to get back out. As soon as I went to opt out and turned him, he lost his footing and went over. I dunno how deep it was, but I was fully clad with oilcoat on an' all – leggings, the lot. So I had to get away from him as quick as I could. I was lucky I got a kick off the saddle otherwise he would have clobbered me. My brother was following down parallel and he reckoned that I was just clear of his flying hooves. I got to the stage where I couldn't have gone any further. If one stroke was going to save my life I couldn't have made it. The power just goes out of your arms. Then my boot hit the beach. The horse was drowned. I got out and he didn't.

dairy factory

Most people made a bit of butter and sent it away on the trading vessel whenever it came down. Of course my dad was one of them, not that my uncle Paddy was ever very keen on the dairying side of it, or the whitebaiting side of it for that matter. He was more of a straight-out stockman, he liked the Hereford cattle and the runs and that sort of thing. But my dad was keen to get the dairy factory going, which he did, and then branched on to making cheese. I think the most cows we milked was about 160 or 170. It was quite a big operation. Some of the cheese went to London. He got first grade on the London market for some of it. It wasn't hard to sell, it was good cheese, I can remember it. While the cheese was being made, we always had a proper cheesemaker. But it didn't carry on for that many years. Generally he had two or three men employed milking the cows.

It was a hard place to run an industry like that, with the way the shipping service was. It was very irregular. If you wanted parts and things, there was no air service or anything like that. It could take from a fortnight to a month or two months, sometimes even more, to get parts. People had to be very self-reliant. My dad was a jack of all trades, you know, part-time mechanic and everything like that. There wasn't anyone else much to turn to. They used to get the engineer on the boat to come up for any knotty mechanical problem. He was one of the few mechanics who used to visit the district.

whitebaiting

Right from when I was a small kid I can remember it [whitebait] streaming up the rivers, you know. People couldn't do any more with it than just eat what they wanted. There was no refrigeration, you couldn't keep it or anything. My dad could see possibilities in canning them. He went to Sydney, bought some machinery for canning and started up the canning factory up here, where he'd previously had the dairy factory.

From there it started, in a small way of course. There was a lot of teething troubles with the canning. In those days he actually imported the cans but after a few years he went back over to Sydney and got the can-making equipment. We made our own cans here then. There was a terrible lot of work before the season even started, making these cans. It would be six weeks or even a couple of months making these cans in the tail end of the winter.

It was about a seven-man operation to make the cans. And about the same to can the whitebait. They came in sheets of ten, about three foot long by two foot wide, I suppose. The first operation was the

Nolans' whitebait factory at Okuru 1929– 1963.
Courtesy of Bill Nolan

guillotine to stamp out appropriate pieces. Then there was a curving roller, that sort of made it round. Then there was another intricate machine – it put a bit of a hook on either end of the can, and you had to hook these together and put these in another machine and stamp your foot! Then they had to be all soldered. Terrible lot of work. There was another one, it used to be called the flanger, it would put a flange on them. There was another separate machine that would stamp out the lids. Another machine was a seamer, it would seam the two together. It was high speed and the most intricate of the

Bill Nolan (Des's eldest brother) processing whitebait, c. 1940. Courtesy of Bill Nolan

machines. If you were slightly out in any separate operation, you could throw that one away in the box. It was useless.

We had these trap nets going and you know, one on each side of the river used to just about cater for the catching part of it. Of course, this was in the one-man one-river days. I fished the Waiatoto for about five years and that's where I caught the record catch, 130 kerosene tins in a day. It was 1944. There was a shortage of tin, the motor vessel, the *Gael*, couldn't get in. There were fine spells of weather but not enough water in the river. The river mouth wasn't suitable for the boat to work. The boat couldn't come down and we ran right out of this tin plate. We tried to get it flown by Captain Mercer, but he couldn't fly it. One of his planes crashed on the glacier at that time, which didn't help. My two brothers, Kevin and Eddie, had to take a pack-train of ten horses through to Paringa. They got the tin carted down to there by road service and then carted it over the Paringa Saddle, ten packloads of tin. Terrible to-do really.

Whitebait wars? I think wherever there was whitebait

Robbie Nolan (brother of Des) working the tin seaming machine.
Courtesy of Bill Nolan

that happened. Henry Buchanan started up sort of in opposition. Things gradually developed and I think in a mild term you could call it a bit of whitebait war. When the flying came in, well that more or less did away with the canning because there was too much labour involved with the canning compared with flying it. It was just so easy to fly them out and put them on the railhead at Hokitika and over to the Christchurch market.

I honestly think myself that the whitebait are getting caught out, but if you ask a dozen or twenty people I suppose they would all just about come up with a different theory on it. That's what whitebaiting is like. But I think weight of numbers has told on it. The last two seasons for instance have been very poor. I think the weight of fishing has told, there are not enough getting away to breed. It's anyone's guess what the coming season is going to be, which it always is of course, but they have definitely gone off in a pretty big way.

flying

I was always keen to have a go at flying. I actually applied to the Air Force during the Second World War but I was always second grade with various blooming medical problems. At that stage they wouldn't have anything to do with anyone who was second grade. So there was no way I could learn to fly until after the war was over and the aeroclubs came back. I went to Christchurch with the idea of learning. I went solo in fourteen lessons – four hours, forty minutes dual instruction.

I would have been something like twenty-six or so when I got my licence. I flew the whitebait I suppose for seven or eight years. I flew them out of the Cascade for five years for the Buchanans, buying off them. In 1950 our firm got a Miles Messenger, a low-wing monoplane. It was very good taking off with loads but it was really the wrong construction, you know, being wood and glue on the West Coast. I didn't realise that a low-wing is not the thing for the West Coast – you are too close to the muddy ground.

The weather, the cloud and the fog and the murk, that was the biggest problem. Strong winds and cross winds on the airstrip, all that. Oh yes, I had quite a few frights. There was one in particular which was a real hair raiser. Of course it was a bit of a mistake on my part as the pilot – I should have turned back.

I was going out from here, it was just a couple of days before Christmas. I had a Hokitika bloke that worked here, name of Stevens. Well, he was going out with me. We were going to leave about nine

Des Nolan, pilot, c. 1947.
Courtesy of Bill Nolan

or ten in the morning but it was one of those wet days. I got the forecast from Hokitika and it was no good. I decided I would postpone it temporarily, see what the afternoon was like, you see. It went to the southwest and it cleared up quite good, even blue sky. So after an hour or two I got another report from Hokitika which still wasn't very good at all. So we decided to leave. It was good as gold up to the Okarito Lagoon – and there it was, like a great wall, cloud and murk, fog right down. Well, very very foolishly, I suppose it was one of the big mistakes of my time flying, I said to Merl, 'I'll have a look in and see what it's like.' Well, it was a great mistake. I should have turned back into Franz, it was the obvious thing to do.

I wasn't long in the damn stuff, when it was so bad I couldn't turn back. I missed my chance at the mouth of the Wanganui River – I could have turned there. I was battling to keep visual contact with the foreshore and the rocks and what have you, the bluffs. It got that bad that I said to Merl, 'I don't think there's much use in turning back now.' It couldn't get much worse than what we were going through. Well shortly after that I just lost everything. I was poking along there with the compass. I didn't know what to do really. There was no hope of turning, I couldn't even see anything. I started edging into the right shore side, which of course was obviously the wrong thing to do, but I had to do something. Then I heard this blood curdling half-scream half-roar from Merl. I was half expecting it really. I didn't see a thing myself. I just whipped into a steep turn to the left and dropped my altitude as I went. I was flying absolutely blind, and halfway through the turn I looked over my right shoulder and there's big tree trunks rushing straight at us and huge rocks, half as big as a house, and a whole lot of kiekies and things. It's amazing how much you can take in with one quick glance. Well, close, I dunno how close but I've never been able to give us more than one second. The next thing we are flying out over the sea, which was a hell of a relief to be able to see something. If I hadn't of dropped altitude in the turn – well, we were shot; that was one of the things that saved us, plus Merl screaming out. I went well out as far as I could, keeping in contact with coast, having had one hell of a fright with the bluff. It always improved from what we called Boulder Head below Ross. And sure enough we got an improvement there and we got through and made it. It was close, by God it was close! I suppose nearly all pilots do this some time or another – you know, an indiscretion. You know you've made a mistake.

It was round about the time that the road came through that I knocked off, actually. It wasn't so important then to have and to maintain an aeroplane. It would have been handy just the same of course, but with running my own farm and that sort of thing, one way and another it wasn't on.

motels

Eileen was keen to start a motel, which she did. She built them one at a time more or less. We had four units then. There was hardly anything else in that line in the district. They were in demand; it was quite a good sideline, really. Different today with all the opposition. It must have been about 1960 we started, that was when the Haast Road went through. It was another five years before the road from Haast to Paringa was open – that was 1965. She had the motels, plus she ran a whitebait-buying business as well and that was more of a thriving industry than what it is today.

[What was it like for a woman to marry into the district?] I think it was a shock to the system in a lot of ways. Townspeople find that generally, I think. I've always said, it was not an easy place for a woman to live. Depending on what their interests are and all that. A lot of social life they miss out on and that sort of thing. It's more of an outdoor sort of an existence that suits men a lot better. You've got deer shooting and

Des and Eileen (née Maunsell), who were married in 1953. Courtesy of Bill Nolan

85

fishing and a lot of different outdoor pursuits that men can have as hobbies, but not too many for women.

crime
It just didn't happen down here. I can't remember any serious crime. There might have been the odd little bit of cattle rustling done here and there but it was only on a very small scale ... Of course all small districts, they all have their squabbles. That happens everywhere and this place was no exception of course.

cattle farming
It is vastly different. You see, you couldn't sell this side of Whataroa, they had to be all driven to the saleyards up there. Of course once the road got through that was the end of the cattle drives. The Paringa Road, it was a hazard really. You always used to have no less than about six drovers to drive something like about 180 head. Each man would have about thirty-five head of cattle on those bad sections of road. The Whataroa end was forgotten about once the Haast Pass Road got through. Then when the road opened up the coast in 1965 we went back to trucking them up there again. Sometimes half each way or some would send their cattle out to Cromwell and some to Whataroa. It was a lot easier certainly than droving them out on the horses. Now we have our own saleyards down here, on the Turnbull. Nearly all the cattle here are sold at the local saleyards. Big crowds of people come mainly from the Otago side and from up the coast.

We were always conscious of the isolation, certainly. But on the other hand, you didn't miss it somehow. You might say that we didn't know any different. That was the way things were and everyone was quite happy, you know. There was no great dissatisfaction about it that I can remember.

You know, convenience of travel, being able to travel up and down in your car, that sort of thing makes it, I suppose you could say, a different place to live. Packhorse mail, you couldn't get anything much more primitive, so you might say that now we are on a footing with the rest of New Zealand.

Des Nolan mustering cattle in the Okuru Valley.
From The New Zealanders in Colour *by Kenneth and Jean Bigwood*

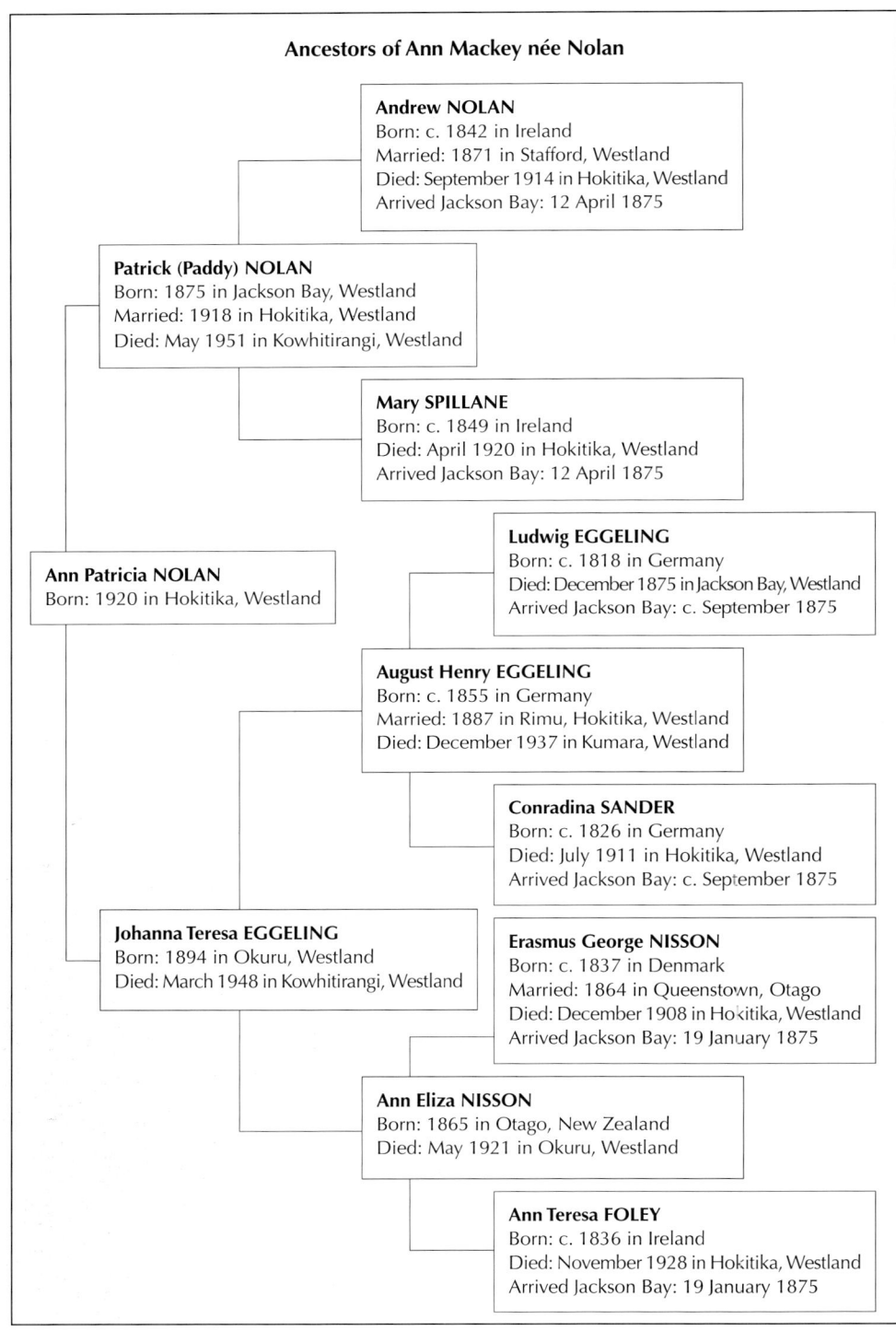

Ancestors of Ann Mackey née Nolan

Andrew NOLAN
Born: c. 1842 in Ireland
Married: 1871 in Stafford, Westland
Died: September 1914 in Hokitika, Westland
Arrived Jackson Bay: 12 April 1875

Patrick (Paddy) NOLAN
Born: 1875 in Jackson Bay, Westland
Married: 1918 in Hokitika, Westland
Died: May 1951 in Kowhitirangi, Westland

Mary SPILLANE
Born: c. 1849 in Ireland
Died: April 1920 in Hokitika, Westland
Arrived Jackson Bay: 12 April 1875

Ludwig EGGELING
Born: c. 1818 in Germany
Died: December 1875 in Jackson Bay, Westland
Arrived Jackson Bay: c. September 1875

Ann Patricia NOLAN
Born: 1920 in Hokitika, Westland

August Henry EGGELING
Born: c. 1855 in Germany
Married: 1887 in Rimu, Hokitika, Westland
Died: December 1937 in Kumara, Westland

Conradina SANDER
Born: c. 1826 in Germany
Died: July 1911 in Hokitika, Westland
Arrived Jackson Bay: c. September 1875

Johanna Teresa EGGELING
Born: 1894 in Okuru, Westland
Died: March 1948 in Kowhitirangi, Westland

Erasmus George NISSON
Born: c. 1837 in Denmark
Married: 1864 in Queenstown, Otago
Died: December 1908 in Hokitika, Westland
Arrived Jackson Bay: 19 January 1875

Ann Eliza NISSON
Born: 1865 in Otago, New Zealand
Died: May 1921 in Okuru, Westland

Ann Teresa FOLEY
Born: c. 1836 in Ireland
Died: November 1928 in Hokitika, Westland
Arrived Jackson Bay: 19 January 1875

Chapter 8

'The only other girl in my life was my sister'

Ann Mackey

Ann (née Nolan) was born at Hokitika in August 1920, her mother, Johanna (née Eggeling), having travelled up from Haast for the birth of her second daughter. Ann and her older sister, Maria, grew up on the family farm at Okuru. In the early 1940s Paddy and Johanna Nolan sold their farm to Paddy's brother, Denis (Din), who farmed the land in partnership with his sons. Paddy and Johanna bought a dairy farm at Kowhitirangi and were assisted in the running of it by Ann and her husband, Harold Mackey. Ann and Harold stayed on the farm until 1971, when they retired to Blenheim. The couple have five children.

my first journey to Haast

My first experience of a horse was when I was carried overland from Whataroa, or it could have been Ross, to Okuru. My mother went to Hokitika to have me, and she was supposed to come back on the *Elsie*, but for some reason it was delayed, or she'd just missed it, and it wasn't going for two or three months. My mother felt she should get back, so they decided that my father would come up and get mother and me. Then the problem was how were they were going to carry a six-week-old baby

Ann Mackey (née Nolan), 1998. Courtesy of Ann Mackey

home. My father came up with the idea of using an old dress basket and carried me in front of him on the horse. That was my introduction to horse riding that I cannot remember.

my mother

My mother was a marvellous boatwoman. She used to ferry people across the Okuru River whether it was in flood or not. She

sat by her kitchen window where she could see across the Okuru River, and she always knew if people were there. If she heard a shot in the middle of the night, she'd get up, get us kids up, take a rug with us, take us down to where the boat landing was, wrap us in rugs and put us under ferns and say, 'Now you girls stay there. I won't be very long. I'll just bring these people over.' They'd come over, and she'd bring them home for a cup of tea irrespective of who they were.

Paddy Nolan and Johanna Eggeling on their wedding day, 1918.
Courtesy of Ann Mackey

Why she was such a good oarswoman was that her family, when they were growing up, had to row across the Turnbull River to go to the school at Okuru. She couldn't swim, and I don't know why they weren't drowned because they used to go out into the middle of the river and start rocking it to see how far over it could go, but the good Lord up top looked after them all.

my father

My father was an older man, and he used to be away from home quite often because they farmed at the Cascade, and those days he'd go away for stretches of six to eight weeks at a time. Looking back, I think what a lonely life my poor mum must have had.

Dad was marvellous with the cattle. He'd drive the cattle for the Nolan brothers from Cascade to the saleyard at Whataroa. He used to recite a lot of Banjo Paterson poems; he had loads of poetry books. One time during the slump days in the 1930s, the cattle weren't selling very well, and he said, 'Well, I'm not driving them all the way back.' It was thirty shillings for a great big beast. He got on the saleyards, and he said, 'It's only a pound. Who'll give me a pound?' And he recited that whole poem of Banjo Paterson's, and that started the bidding.

My father, if anyone was sick, he would chop wood for them; he was a very generous man. Prior to my time, he done a very brave thing. He had rescued three men at Bruce Bay. They were told not to go out in this little rowboat, but they would defy everyone and went out and the boat capsized. My father got someone's horse, a little pony it was, and he made the horse go into the sea three times to rescue these men. He used to put them onto the horse and hang onto the horse's mane with his teeth and make it swim, and of course the horse was very tired battling the big waves by the time he got out to the third man. He lost one of the stirrups, and after saving a son of one of the men on the shore whose horse it was, he got told off for losing the stirrup. After saving the son!

A gallant rescue	… Be it understood that Nolan measures 6ft 2″ in height and weighs 14 stone. The pony he rode is only 14 hands high. On one trip the pony got exhausted and would have sunk but Nolan promptly got off his back and swam alongside him. Such pluck and coolness, Mr Editor, is deserving of the highest praise, and I hope the agent of the Humane Society will make a note of it for he certainly deserves the medal as he undeniably saved the three men's lives. Nor are they the only lives he has saved, for when a lad he rushed into the Okuru River with all his clothing on and rescued his two younger brothers, who were being swept away.
	Henry Morrison, surveyor, from Gillespies Beach, to the editor of the *West Coast Times* 28 March 1900
	Paddy Nolan was awarded a silver medal by the Royal Humane Society of New Zealand in March 1908.

my grandad

I can only remember my grandad on my mother's side, Grandad Eggeling. He used to sit on our verandah, and he'd be rubbing his knees because he had arthritis, and he'd say, 'My poor knees, my poor knees.' He was a marvellous man. He made little wheelbarrows out of wood for us, and they were all hand done, and he made whistles out of branches from trees. We just thought he was marvellous.

I wasn't very old, but I can remember my Grandfather Eggeling when he lived in his old home over at the Turnbull. He used to catch these birds and stuff them. He had all these stuffed birds, and we loved nothing better than going in to see these birds because quite a few of them had disappeared, but they were all there in his old dairy. That's another thing: my Grandfather Eggeling used to make his own smoked saveloys.

our house

We lived in a wooden house built up off the ground. Quite often floods would come right through there and sweep everything clean. It had a verandah right around it like the old-style houses did. We had a kitchen with a wood stove and an open fireplace. Some of the cooking was done in a camp oven on the open fire.

We used to boil up the water in the copper to have

baths – an old tin bath in front of the fire in the kitchen. If we had a long dry spell, the pump would go dry, and I can remember my sister and I and my mother, we used to carry buckets of water up from the river, and we had to come up this steep bank. We used to wash up in a tin dish until we got a sink. I would have been about ten or twelve when we got a sink to wash up in. That was a godsend.

I reckon mother made the nicest scones. Her and Auntie Norah Cron – there'd be a toss up who made the nicest scones. And she baked all her own bread. If Dad was going away on these cattle treks to the saleyards or going to the Cascade for a good length of time, she'd be up baking bread until two or three in the morning. She made a yeast out of potatoes. It was cut up raw and sugar added and left to ferment. When it started to froth up, that would be the time to bottle it and cork it down and leave it for about ten days. You'd hear all these corks popping. Some of the bottles blew to pieces, and there'd be yeast smell everywhere. That was the yeast they used till later on when they used to get compressed yeast by the mail, but sometimes it was blue and gone off by the time you got it.

The supplies for the bread, the flour and sugar were bought in bulk. They had to order it in bulk because the boat only came in every three months. If the weather was bad and the bar was blocked and it couldn't get in, well you just waited and waited until it was able to come in. Oh yes! [It was a big event.] We all gathered around to see the unloading. The boat unloaded the produce that came in: the flour, the sugar, the raisins, wheat, pollard bran. You name it, they brought it – tea, coffee, anything. Then they'd load the butter on, to take it back to Hokitika, and whatever produce they had. They might have sent out timber; I forget now. In later years they tried to send the cattle beasts out, but it wasn't a success because by the time they reached market, having been two or three days at sea without food or water, they were not in a good condition for sale.

There were no mod cons. The womenfolk would do their sewing, they'd do their knitting, they'd do their darning and mending, and all that sort of thing in the evenings. I'm not sure what the menfolk done. My father used to read his poems. He had a fantastic memory. He could recite poem after poem without making one mistake. He could put expression into them and make them come alive. The 'Man from Snowy River' and all those sorts of poems; mostly Banjo Paterson. That was his relaxation. He would also be out chopping wood, and it was our job to bring that in. We had plenty of chores.

doing the washing

The washing was done in tubs and a copper. Every Sunday night my mother soaked the clothes. She'd fill the tub with water, and she'd get the soap and scrub the clothes on the old washing board – a glass washing board, if you please. When she'd decided it was clean enough,

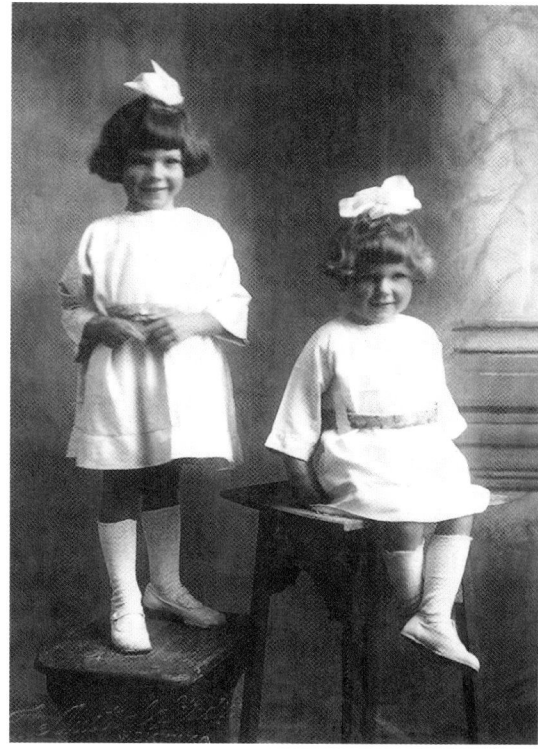

Ann Nolan (right) with her older sister Maria, c. 1924.
Courtesy of Ann Mackey

it was tossed into the copper, and it was boiled in there. When it was finished boiling, she'd fish it out with the copper stick. When the clothes had been boiled enough, you'd fill the tub again with cold water; you'd put the clothes in there and then put them through a wringer, and they'd go into another tub of cold water with Reckitts Blue in it. She'd wring them from there, and then they'd be hung out on the clothesline to dry. Then they'd come in, and they'd be folded up. Ones that had to be starched would be separated before they went out on the clothesline, and they went into a kerosene tin full of starch that had been made up. Everything was ironed; all the underclothing was ironed. The irons had to be heated up. Mother had one made of cast iron with a handle, and you stoked the fire up and heated them in front of the coals. You grabbed the handle of the iron with a pot-holder and dusted the ash off with a rag, and then used it for your ironing. If it was too hot, you scorched your clothes, and that was a big disaster. If it wasn't hot enough to iron the starched things, that was another disaster. It was trial and error. However, that's how I learned to iron. As I got older, we graduated to a petrol iron, which was really dangerous. They could blow up, and you'd get dreadful burns from them.

Christmas time

Come Christmas time we'd have to round up all these young geese and kill the goslings for Christmas dinner, and that'd take a full day – to get the geese, chop their heads off, pluck them. You'd pluck the feathers off, and all the feathers were saved. Then they were plunged into a copper of hot water to get all the down off, and I've an idea that that was dried out too and saved. The feathers and down were made into quilts; that was a winter's job. Then you would build a big bonfire – well, not too big, you needed lots of blaze – but not too fierce, and you'd hold your plucked goose over that to singe it. Then when you'd got all that done, everyone would come and get their Christmas goose.

Christmas Day was a real event to us. Mother had two brothers [Charlie and Dick], and at this time they were single. They came lots of times to visit us, and there was a crack in the ceiling, and one used to say, 'See Santa Claus is up there looking down at you, and if you're naughty, he won't bring you any presents.' Of course we really and truly believed in fairies and goodness knows what in those days. He was the biggest tease. Christmas Day was an event. My mother would be baking for days.

Santa Claus was a big thing to us. It was the only time we ever got anything. We usually got a new dress and new shoes at Christmas, and Santa Claus brought us a doll or a cake of soap. We'd try and keep awake to see Santa Claus come, but naturally we never did. We'd get an orange, a banana and an apple. You'd get peanuts in a shell, and you'd save them. You'd save your lollies. You'd cut them into bits so you would have some for later on. You'd save everything. Christmas doesn't mean the same to me now; there was something magic about it [then].

We always had goose or something like that for Christmas; Paradise ducks when they were there. You'd catch them as flappers. What fun we had catching flappers! A flapper is a duck just before it can fly. You'd get amongst them, and you'd have a ball of fun. That was our relaxation. My mother was a great shot. In those days you were allowed to shoot pigeons, and pigeon soup was just out of this world. When they were on the miro berries, they were so lovely – but you didn't touch them when they on the kowhai because the taste of the leaves went into them, and they weren't very nice at all.

a day out

In those days we had horse races down at Mussel Point, and the Condons used to come down, and the Williams used to come down from the Fox Glacier – Weheka it was called. This was always at Easter time, and my mother used to bake biscuits and seal them in great big tins so she'd have them there, and she wouldn't have to be baking, and she could go to the day at the races. I can't remember much about that, but I do remember the Condon girls, and there was a Nellie Breeze used to come down there. They used to have these beautiful glass bangles on, and we used to love these, not being able to get to any shops or anything like that. You have no idea. I was sixteen before I actually can remember seeing a train.

I remember my father saying – I think it was when his sister, Norah Cron, was getting married – they took all the hay out to hold the dance in the barn for them. Then after the wedding was over, it looked like rain, so they had to turn around and put all the hay back into the barn. No, there wasn't many weddings in my day, but in earlier days

Paddy Nolan, c. 1930.
Alexander Turnbull Library/Te Puna Matauranga o Aotearoa, C – 23481/-1/2.

94

apparently there was. It used to be a standing joke that when the priest or minister of religion came down they did the christening and the wedding at the same time.

the rivers

One time my father was coming home from the Cascade with his workmate Len Johanson and they got as far as the Hapuka. The bridge had been washed out there, so they went to ford the river. The tide was in. The thunder and lightning was such that the horses went into

the river so far and then turned around and went back. It was so dark that my father thought they had got across the river, but when the next lot of lightning came he could see they were back on the same side they started from. He decided that the best thing to do was to tie the horses up and crawl under a flax bush. They were soaking wet, and he said that all night he heard Len say, 'I've never been so cold in all my life. I've never been so cold in all my life.'

Everything was based on tides. When they were going to the Cascade, they had to catch the tide at the Turnbull River, at the Waiatoto River and at the Arawhata River. But normally they just went from home to the Arawhata; they didn't do the Cascade in one day.

You used a boat if it was high tide and you wanted to ferry. You put the saddles and the dogs in the boat with you, and the horses swam behind the boat. You had to be very careful because sometimes the horses want to take charge of a boat, and I remember, when I was young, mother wasn't able to go this day, and I said, 'Well, I will go and ferry them across.' I went down, and I launched the boat, and I got over all right. It was the minister and his wife. Before they got in the boat, I unsaddled the horses and put the saddles in the boat, and they sat in the stern end. I said, 'The river has got a strong current here. Whatever you do, don't let the horses take charge because I can't row against horses. Don't let them get up by me where the oars are. Just smack them on the nose with the end of your bridle and keep them close behind the boat.' When you are not used to that sort of thing, I suppose it is very difficult, and the lady let her horse take charge, and I had quite a difficult time with it, and in the end I told her to let it go. I said, 'It'll follow the other horse', and that's what happened. There was all those little things that you had to watch out for; you had to be very aware of all sorts of safety measure. Oh … I was about twelve. My mother used to take us out rowing. She used to row down to the bar, which was a good two-and-a-half miles away.

visitors

Oh, Bill O'Leary [Arawata Bill], he used to come riding up our driveway. Ho, ho or something he'd say. He always carried a stick, and he had a hat on, and he'd throw the hat up into the air and onto his stick. We loved it when Bill O'Leary came because he always brought us strawberries. We'd run down to meet him, and he'd grab us by the hand, and he'd pull us up, and he'd put me on front and Maria at the back or vice versa, and we'd get a ride home. He'd come in: 'How's the Missus today? Have you got a cup of tea for us?'

We were like this: little girls should be seen but not heard. If the adults had anything they thought our ears were too tender to hear, we were shooed outside; we weren't allowed in. So we grew up with that. We had no confidence. It all had been knocked out of us. I can thank my husband for me getting that confidence back. When I was eighteen, if anyone spoke to me, I would go as red as a beetroot. Talk about bush-rats. I've heard it put very nicely and politely that the West Coast people are very inhibited, and I would go along with that. People would come there, and we were so shy that we'd run away and hide, Maria and I. We'd run to our bedrooms or run into the bush to hide. You've no idea what it was like. Yet it was all right with the ones we knew.

the mail

Our mail came in by horseback, and we were expecting these nice velvet dresses that my mother was getting made for us in Ross. They came, and of course the packhorse had to be swum across flooded rivers, and the dye had run. But still, they were new dresses, and we thought they were marvellous because living down there you didn't get very much new.

Charlie Smith , the mailman, was very easy going; a placid man. He treated everyone the same. He was a nice old man. He took everything in his stride. Nothing ruffled him. He must have taken some hellfire risks. He got told off if the mail was wet, but it wasn't always his fault. And you know, to travel that once a fortnight—how monotonous, what a tedious thing. They wouldn't do it today. Rain, hail or shine the mail must go through, and my God he was very seldom late. If he was a day late, that was a disaster. If he was two days late, that was the end of the world!

Charlie Smith, the mailman, leaving Cowans' house at Okuru, c. 1930. Weekly News 22 March 1933

getting an
education

I honestly do think my father, my mother and that generation got a better education than we did because the settlement was at the start and they had teachers there. Lily Nolan [a cousin] would have been taught locally, and then she started teaching us in what they called a household school. Later I went to the school at Okuru.

Our [school] lunch wasn't very appetising; it was usually bread and jam sandwiches. Meat and chutney sandwiches were a real treat. Bread and jam sandwiches wrapped in newspaper, can you imagine it? Yuk! I would no more give my kids bread and jam sandwiches than fly!

First my teacher was Mr Hector Brown; he boarded at Mrs Cowan's place. There wasn't many of us at school. I think there were four Harrises, Cath and Bernie Cowan, Maria and myself and the five Nolan boys. Then Mr Brown left, and we had to wait a long time to get another teacher, and we had no education in that space of time. Then a Miss Bostridge came. Fancy a girl coming from a town like Greymouth to an out of the way place like Okuru where there was fortnightly mail and no transport. It must have been a terrible thing. They couldn't go out for their holidays. They went out for Christmas because that was six weeks, but other times they had to stay there.

Infantile paralysis – or as they now term it, polio – broke out. All schools were closed, so we were without a teacher I think for about six months. Then Mr Gillan was appointed, and he stayed for the rest of my school career. He always compared us kids with kids that he had taught in Greymouth, and of course we were the worst kids. We were always put down. You took it as the norm that you didn't rate very highly at all.

Some of the people were dissatisfied with Mr Gillan's teaching, so someone decided to set up in opposition. To avoid controversy my mother decided that she would take Maria and I away from school. My mother didn't want to get involved; all the Eggelings were very placid people. Therefore I left school at the age of twelve. I still have my proficiency certificate at home. I treasure that very much indeed. I suppose I have taught myself a lot since I left school.

Not being sent to high school? That made me feel pretty awful. Cath Cowan went, of course. Her mother was a city girl. She came from Christchurch. On looking back, I think it must have been a dreadful upheaval for Marge, Mrs Cowan, coming from the city; she must have wondered what struck her. Anyway, Cath was sent away. The Nolan boys all went over to Oamaru to St Kevin's College, but it was deemed that because we were girls, we didn't need to have an education, because we would grow up and get married. I mean I felt pretty terrible about that, and in my teen years I thought if only I could, if only I could. I vowed and declared at a very young age that if ever I had a family, that irrespective if

Ann Nolan at her Okuru home at the age of fifteen.
Courtesy of Ann Mackey

they were boys or girls, they would get the best education I could afford.

I didn't realise until I came out to Kowhitirangi and my girls were at school that I knew absolutely nothing about sports. I couldn't play tennis! Women in my age group had done all these things. I hadn't done anything! When I brought my girls home, I would get them to explain the game to me. When we played games at school, there wasn't enough of us to play much.

When my mother was younger, she went up to Hokitika and found work at the Seaview Mental Hospital, and that's where most people made for, but my desire was to be a dressmaker, and I would have done anything to have been able to have gone away and learnt the trade. But it wasn't to be.

I was terribly lonely. The only other girl in my life was my sister. I had a pretend friend. Now, that might sound silly to you, but it was the loneliness that drove me to that. You see my parents had each other. They were good to us. They used to take us out, and we had lots of chores to do. There was no other girl there except my sister.

water wings and whitebait

My uncle Din Nolan used to get us up, his five boys and Maria and I, at seven o'clock in the morning, and we had to learn to swim. We had to blow up these wings and put them on. Ohh, in the cold morning it wasn't very pleasant, but never mind, we did learn to swim. Then after we had swum, we had to run back up to his place and get on the dumb-bells, and we'd be experts at that; we could swing them around. The boys had to get on the punch bags. That was taboo to the girls.

Uncle Din had a raspberry patch, and after Christmas we'd all be taken down there and have to pick these blooming raspberries.

This went on for about a week, and we'd make all the excuses. Once that was done, it was spud-picking time. We had to pick up the little ones in buckets. It was always by the river, and we'd be making excuses to run down and get a drink, but we were hauled back. It was fun. We daren't throw a potato, my gawd! That would be it.

My sister and I used to make whitebait nets out of sugarbags. A creek ran round our place. Just an old creek, full of old logs and bits and pieces, and Maria and I used to go out there with our homemade whitebait nets and catch these whitebait. The eels would be supping away at them. When the sacks were full, we'd drag the whitebait up onto the bank, throw it out onto the bank, and skate through them and then let the chooks feed on them. That was our fun, and climbing trees and bird-nesting. There was great competition between the Nolan boys and us two girls to see who got the most. We had all sorts of eggs.

Ann and her mother whitebaiting some time during the 1930s. Courtesy of Bill Nolan

health

My mother had trouble having babies. She lost a daughter after me from the mere fact that there was no medical care. The baby was born healthy enough, but the cord had been cut too close to the navel or something, and the little girl haemorrhaged, and they didn't know what to do about it. By the time Sister Gunn got there, the baby was dead, but they said that if they'd put a raisin in there, it would have stopped the bleeding. But of course no one knew.

If anyone got sick down there, they had to build a stretcher. A stretcher was made out of two poles of wood with four handles and a bit of canvas or old wheat-sack or something tacked or sewn onto it. That was what they called a stretcher. They organised the menfolk; they had relays. I think it was twelve horses and twelve men, and four of the men were carrying. Every so many minutes they changed around, and this is how they did it, in a relay all the way through like that. I think the last one that was carried out was Saunders; you know, he was down the pit there, and his face was smashed. He would have been the last one because the next time it was by plane.

They had the telephone when it wasn't down. They could get in contact with a nurse or a doctor to see whether it was necessary to take the patient out or not. The line would be cut off for weeks. A tree might have blown over it, and then they'd have to find the break to begin with, which might take two or three days. The roadman was usually at Copper Creek or the Iron Hut or Paringa. There wasn't one at each of those places; there was only one at either place. He would have to go right through to find the break. We never had the telephone on. That's another thing – I was really scared of telephones.

My teeth rotted in my head because there was no dental service down there. I had to come out when I was about fourteen to Hokitika, and unfortunately I had to have all my top teeth extracted. Until you have dentures, you don't know what it is like not to be able to bite into an apple, not to be able to chew on a bone. Toothache! You'd be kept up all night; you would be in agony. You'd have great abscesses. How we weren't poisoned, I don't know. You could see the holes in your teeth. You'd roll up cotton-wool buds and stick them in the iodine bottle and stick them in your tooth. You were doing that all night. After a few days, when the abscess broke, everything was okay for a wee while, and then it would start up again. My uncle, Din Nolan, used to extract teeth, but I chickened out; I couldn't have it done. To lose your teeth at that age is a dreadful thing. I was without teeth for twelve months before I could get back to Hokitika to get the plate made.

air service

The working bee at Mussel Point, making an airstrip for the first aeroplane to land in the Haast district, 1931. Courtesy of Paul Beauchamp Legg

Another big event in my life while I lived at Okuru was Tiny White coming in, in the first aeroplane. All the settlers of Okuru spent days making the airstrip. Kids and all were grubbing tussock, filling in rabbit holes. Then the great day arrived. We had to go with the tide to get over there, and we took a picnic lunch. When we saw this little silver dot coming in, well it was fantastic really. A cheer went up. He brought in papers – the *Otago Daily Times*. It was really a fantastic day.

With the aeroplane, the isolation was gone. I remember I was helping Dad along the Waiatoto Beach in the early hours of the morning. We were droving cattle or sheep or something, and Bert Mercer spotted us and threw the paper out to us. We sat down and read the paper, and when we got back, we could tell them all the news. It was fantastic; you didn't feel isolated any more.

The first bicycle, Dick Eggeling brought that home, and that was a novelty. He learnt to ride. I didn't learn to ride until I was fifteen, and oh my God, the spills I had off it! However, I was determined to learn. Once we had the aeroplane, and the boats were coming into Jackson Bay, that's when people started to bring motor vehicles into the district. I can remember the Nolan boys having a motorcycle, and the Ministry of Works, they brought their trucks in, but that would have been in the late 1930s.

The first aircraft to land, Tiny White with Okuru and Haast locals at Mussel Point, 1931. Courtesy of Bill Nolan

my husband

Harold Mackey was working with the Ministry of Works and when Jackson Bay was opened up, he was sent down there with a few other men to build a town there. His gang of men helped build the aerodromes down there. He lived at Andrew Nolan's old house, that wasn't very far from us, and he used to come and get milk off me, and that's how I met my husband.

We got married, and he went away to the war, and when he got back, we took over my father's farm at Kowhitirangi, and we lived there until 1971 when we moved here [Blenheim] to retire. It was terrible to leave Okuru because we were such a close-knit family down there. Everyone knew everyone else, and you came out, and you knew no one.

Ann and Harold Mackey in Wellington, c. 1943.
Courtesy of Ann Mackey

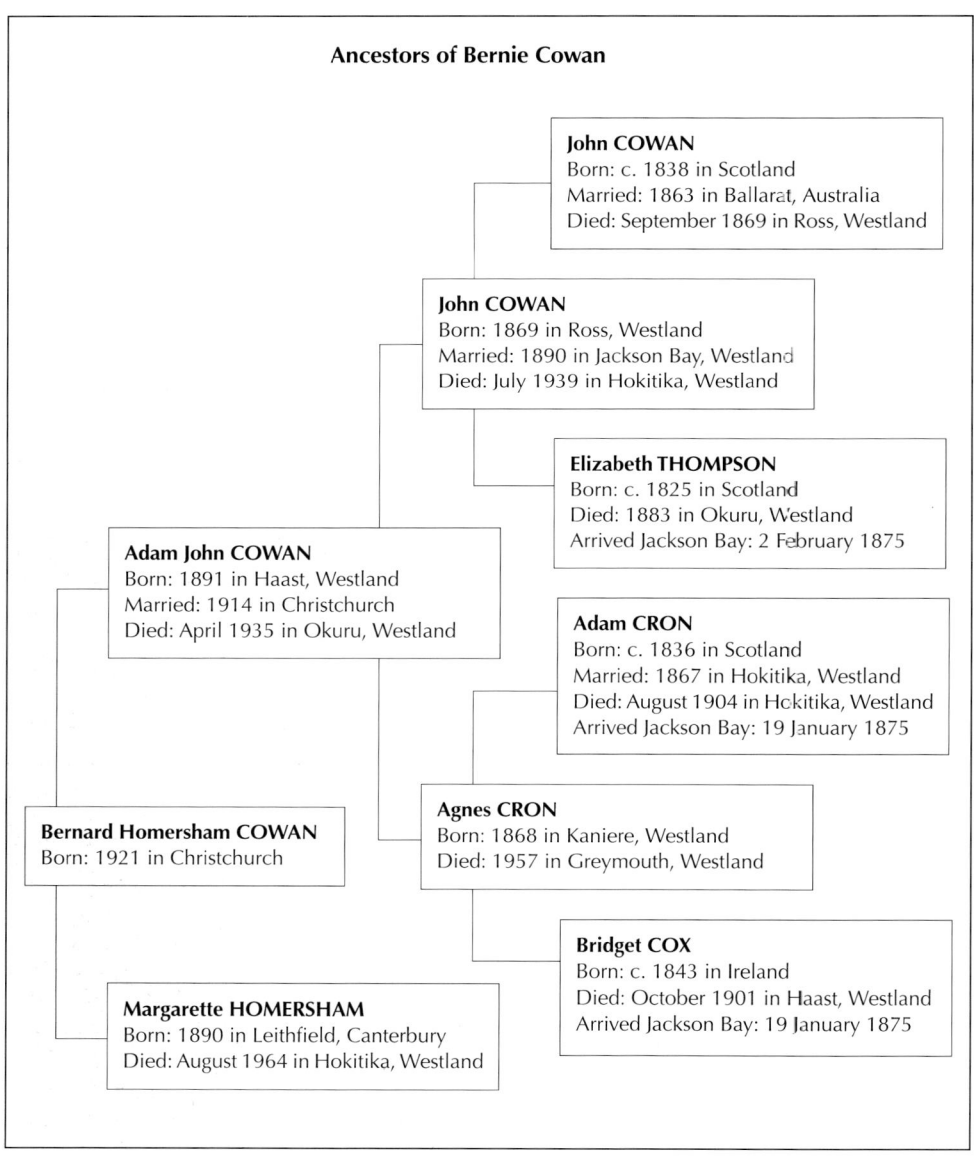

Ancestors of Bernie Cowan

John COWAN
Born: c. 1838 in Scotland
Married: 1863 in Ballarat, Australia
Died: September 1869 in Ross, Westland

John COWAN
Born: 1869 in Ross, Westland
Married: 1890 in Jackson Bay, Westland
Died: July 1939 in Hokitika, Westland

Elizabeth THOMPSON
Born: c. 1825 in Scotland
Died: 1883 in Okuru, Westland
Arrived Jackson Bay: 2 February 1875

Adam John COWAN
Born: 1891 in Haast, Westland
Married: 1914 in Christchurch
Died: April 1935 in Okuru, Westland

Adam CRON
Born: c. 1836 in Scotland
Married: 1867 in Hokitika, Westland
Died: August 1904 in Hokitika, Westland
Arrived Jackson Bay: 19 January 1875

Agnes CRON
Born: 1868 in Kaniere, Westland
Died: 1957 in Greymouth, Westland

Bernard Homersham COWAN
Born: 1921 in Christchurch

Bridget COX
Born: c. 1843 in Ireland
Died: October 1901 in Haast, Westland
Arrived Jackson Bay: 19 January 1875

Margarette HOMERSHAM
Born: 1890 in Leithfield, Canterbury
Died: August 1964 in Hokitika, Westland

Chapter 9

'No such thing as rules and regulations'

Bernie Cowan

Bernie was born in Christchurch in 1921, his mother Margarette (Madge) having travelled from Okuru to her home town for the birth. After the early death of his father, Bernie and his sister, Catherine, ran the small family farm at Okuru. Bernie left the Haast district in 1973, having lived there for fifty-two years, and moved to Christchurch with his wife, Myra. He is a keen gardener and up until recently often travelled to Haast to assist his son, John, on his property. He still hankers to return to the Haast district.

my family

My grandmother was a Cron, that's on my father's side. The family came down and lived at Jackson Bay. My grandmother went to school at Jackson Bay when she was nine years of age. From then on I think the family lived at Haast. After she married, she lived at Okuru. They were there for many years and then left and went to Gillespies Beach. My grandfather helped build a pontoon for a gold dredge there and then they left and came back and lived at Okuru until my grandfather died in

Bernie Cowan, c. 1987. Courtesy of Bernie Cowan

about 1938 or 1939. My grandmother later moved to Greymouth where she lived with my sister. She was nearly ninety when she died.

My father was born at Haast, in the old Haast township out at the front. He showed me one day when we were coming up to Haast in a dray to collect some sheep. He said, 'Son, that's where I was born' and the old chimney was still standing there. It was actually on the north end of the old township in Haast – of course that's all moved to the new town. My mother was born in Leithfield and met my father somewhere in Christchurch. They were married in Christchurch and then went to Okuru.

I was born in Christchurch in 1921 and Mum took me home when I was three months old. We went over to Otira in the coach and then by train from there down to Hokitika. By some means we got from Hokitika down to Franz Josef, which was then called Waiho. It would have been a motor vehicle of some sort, I imagine. Then my father carried me home in a wicker basket on the front of a horse. It was a hundred miles, which took about three days.

my first trip out

I was six when I first went out. We left Okuru and went to Haast and then rode from Haast up to Clarke Hut which was twenty-five miles up the valley. It was the middle of June, absolutely wickedly cold. We stayed the night there and the next day went on to Makarora. From there we went down the lake in the launch to Pembroke. The next day we caught the train at Cromwell to Dunedin. We stayed the night there and then went by train to Christchurch, stayed with some friends of Mum and Dad's and then went to Wellington in the old *Wahine*. I thought it was marvellous seeing big ships like that, they seemed tremendous to me. The big city was well … you can't take it all in.

I think we went up there after my brother [John] died: I think Mum and Dad needed a bit of a break. My brother got ill, he had a bit of pain and was vomiting. The *Elsie* was in at Okuru at the time but the weather was bad and they couldn't go. It was there two or three days. They went when they could get out, but my brother died at about Bruce Bay, about thirty-five miles up the coast, and the boat came back. It was bad news. He should have been carried out right from the word go but my grandmother thought it was just a bit of tummy trouble and gave him a dose of castor oil.

stretchered out

I was actually carried out in a stretcher once. When I was twelve years of age I had appendix and the planes hadn't really started so the people of Okuru and round about volunteered and took turns at carrying me on the stretcher. They travelled all night with me. They carried me from Okuru to Maitai [Mahitahi], which is about sixty miles. From then on I went by gig to Jacobs River and then by car to Cook River. We had to

Bernie (left) with his brother John and his sister Catherine, c. 1925.
Courtesy of Bernie Cowan

cross that by gig and then a bus was waiting on the other side to take me to Hokitika. I remember the journey very well. My father went part of the way and my grandmother stayed with me all the way; she rode a horse all night.

Another time I went with my mother, she had to go and have a check-up at the sanatorium. My mother had TB and from late 1928 she spent fourteen months at the sanatorium. She came home with a clean bill of health but the doctor said that she must go back up for a check-up and she thought she'd take me as well. We went up in the boat which was about a twenty-four-hour trip. We went to Christchurch for a few weeks and came back to Hokitika. When we got there my father was there – he had to go to hospital with severe sinus trouble. My parents decided to send me home to my grandmother. My mother wasn't very keen about me going on the boat by myself at nine years of age.

shipwrecked on the *Elsie*

We were only about two hours out of Hokitika when the motor first stopped. They got it started and late at night the same day it completely stopped and they couldn't get it going. We just drifted up and down the coast for five days. Skyrockets went off and people saw us, but they didn't take a great deal of notice. Then a terrific northerly got up and the sail got blown away and there was a big sea. She went ashore at two o'clock in the morning – that was in September 1930.

I wasn't frightened because I think you don't realise the danger. There was about five on board altogether. The captain said he had no idea where we were going, we were just getting blown ashore. We were very lucky. Had we been a mile or so further north, we would have gone onto a rock bluff, but we came up on to Hunts Beach, a beautiful sandy beach. The sea broke over the stern of the boat and half-filled the little cabin. Then one of the crew members said, 'Come on Bernard, quick, the captain says up the mast!' So, we hussled along the side of the ship, up the bulwarks and climbed the mast. That was in case she rolled over.

We were carried up on a great wave; we were swept clean up, high and dry, with one great wave. A chap just picked me off the side and ran up the beach with me. Then we just had to wait. They brought stuff ashore and pitched a tent. Early that morning it hailed and rained, changed to sou'west and became very, very cold. The next day two of them set off. They knew where the road would be but they didn't know how far. It was late that afternoon that Jack and Bill Condon and a Mr Wilson came down with horses. We had about five or six miles to ride and I was taken in by Mrs Wilson and given a big hearty meal.

We went from there to Maitai [Mahitahi], to Jack Condon's place, and following day I set off for home with the mailman. We went to Copper Creek and the next day home, so it was a two-day journey. I could hardly stand up when I got there because I was riding on the back hanging onto the old mailman, Charlie Smith.

The ketch Elsie *leaving Hokitika for the last time in September 1930. Bernie's grandfather, John Cowan, took the photo after seeing Bernie off.*
Courtesy of Bernie Cowan

The cargo on the *Elsie*	The largest piece of cargo on the vessel was a cheese vat for Messrs Nolan Bros of Okuru, for whom most of the cargo on the vessel was also consigned. This vat is about 20ft long and 4ft by 3 feet, and weighs about 15 cwt. Mr P. Nolan arrived on the scene yesterday morning and the question of salvaging this was left in his hands. It was considered that the only way to do so would be to dismantle the vat, as otherwise the transport difficulties would be too immense. *Luckily the* Elsie *on her previous trip took all the machinery etc. for the new whitebait canning factory otherwise a most serious position would have been caused Messrs Nolan Bros.* *Hokitika Guardian* and *Evening Star* 19 September 1930

school

I used to walk with my brother up to Mr and Mrs Nolan's home on the Okuru River and they had a household school there. They had five sons and two of their cousins and my brother and myself. My dad went to school at Okuru but that school was burnt down. They later turned the schoolmaster's residence into a school and I went to school there and that's where I ended my school days. I got to standard six, which wasn't very creditable was it? I had no secondary education. Leaving school was my mother, grandmother and grandfather's idea, that I had to do something at home, like milk cows, and going to school well … The schoolteacher and some of the others weren't very happy about losing one of the pupils at the school.

The Cowan family home at Okuru. Bernie is in the middle with his grandmother, Agnes Cowan (née Cron) and his father Adam, c. 1931. Courtesy of Bernie Cowan

home

Our house was only a two-bedroom house with a kitchen and a dining room. Someone called it a lounge but it wasn't a lounge, I can assure you. It was fairly primitive but very comfortable. It was just a typical West Coast square type of house. We had plenty of firewood and my dad milked cows and we had plenty of vegies, plenty of fish, plenty of whitebait and all that sort of thing. After the *Elsie* was wrecked the *Gael* came on the run and we used to get it in every six weeks or two months. It was no problem getting things down, although we went a bit short sometimes. We very seldom ran out of anything, everyone sort of helped each other.

We had a wood range, an old black stove, a Shacklock range. There was plenty of pigeon stew – a lot of people won't like that. One of the old Scotsmen said to me one time, 'You know, Bernie, if it hadn't been for the ducks and the pigeons we would have just about starved.' The few cattle and sheep that people had, they would want to sell them and try and get some sort of revenue. Flounders and yellow-eyed mullet and

The Cowans' house at Okuru surrounded by flood waters.
Courtesy of Bernie Cowan

things like that were caught at the mouths of the rivers, trout in the river. There was no such thing as rules and regulations in those days. If you saw a trout in shallow water, you would shoot it. Other people used to use a bit of gelignite too, that was quite a common thing.

As far as fish went, my dad used to row out to Open Bay Island with the Eggeling brothers – they were all great mates, the three of them. They'd come home with blue cod and groper and fish like that. It was about two and a half miles, I think. They'd go out in a fourteen-foot open boat. On a calm day it was quite safe. They could all swim but there were no lifejackets or anything like that.

My parents were pretty easy going. After my brother died I was sort of a lone star ranger. My sister went to school in Hokitika when she was eight. I was only three then. Whatever Dad said just went, you never back-chatted him or anything like that and Mum was the same. When you were told to do it you did it, and it never did me any harm. I was very close to my parents and my grandparents too. My brother was the apple of my grandmother's eye but when he died she took me under her wing. It was a very lonely life at times. There was the Nolan boys but they were two-and-a-half miles up the road.

my father

My dad used to milk twenty-five cows and make butter by hand. It was a very poor existence. All my dad had in those days were a few cattle that he would sell, and prices were very very poor, and homemade butter. I think it only amounted to £150 for the year. Later on he got a job cutting a few sleepers but he didn't make much out of that. Dad was killed when I was fourteen and that left us in very dire straits. We had fairly high bills to pay, £150 in one place, £75 in another. I remember my sister telling me, 'We've got to pay this off.' And we did. William Perry and Co., they were the grocers in Hokitika. Mr Perry said to my mother, he said,

'Mrs Cowan, I will never ask you for the money.' But we paid it off after Mr Perry died, my sister and I.

My dad had a little small saw-bench that he and a friend built to cut a little bit of timber for building sheds and anything like that. It was Easter Saturday 1935 and he said, 'We'll go out and cut this sleeper up.' It was to make a kennel for this prize dog he had brought for £5 and it was his pride and joy. There was a friend of ours only living a hundred yards up the hill and if only my dad had asked him to come and help, the

---

Settler carried from Okuru to Mahitahi

A wonderful story of good comradeship worthy of the best records of the old digger days comes from South Westland. From the district of Haast comes the story. There Mr Adam Cowan, son of Mr and Mrs John Cowan, well known southern settlers, was taken ill as the result of an old trouble in the head [sinus] and after consultation with friends it was decided to bring the invalid to Hokitika for treatment. A start was made on Monday afternoon from Okuru and Haast was reached that night. On Tuesday morning at 8 o'clock, the sufferer being in a stretcher, carried by four men commenced the long trek to Paringa which was reached at 10 o'clock that night. Those who have ridden along that long road will have an idea of the difficulty of the journey. There were 18 men on horseback accompanying the party and five minute spells at carrying the stretcher were given, Mr P. Nolan being timekeeper and it was a [sic] wonderful how the men dropped off their horses at the call of the time and relieved the bearers. Some kept behind rounding up the horses, and so the weary day passed slowly. Another relay of 18 men met the party on the way and carried on the good work. A stay was made for the night at a hut at Paringa, where 40 people had gathered, some rest of a nature being taken.

Next morning it was found possible to place the sufferer on a horse on a mattress, with a rider behind to hold him and so the seven mile journey was made to Mahitahi. Here a trap was secured and the journey continued to Karangarua, where the sufferer was placed in a motor car and the rest of the journey was made to Hokitika which was reached at 1.30 o'clock on Thursday morning, a distance of 160 miles being covered for the day.

Too much credit cannot be paid to the settlers of the Southern District, who so readily offered their services, and in spite of the hard work entailed, carried their man on the long journey in record time.

The sufferer stood the journey with remarkable fortitude. On arrival at Hokitika he received medical treatment, but it was considered advisable that a visit be made to Christchurch for further attention and he leaves in the morning. Mrs Cowan accompanied her husband during the trying journey, with his father and mother, the latter joining the party at Mahitahi. They cannot adequately express their very great appreciation of the wonderful good work of the settlers in their hour of need.

West Coast Times 28 August 1925

accident wouldn't have happened. But he thought that me being a keen boy of fourteen, it would be okay. He said to me, 'Whatever you do don't let that stick get on the back of the saw, if you do you'll kill me.' And that's exactly what happened. There was no fender or anything. Of course dad didn't know anything about sawing. He put the first cut through, and I pushed the stick back on an angle and pushed it into the back of the saw – and of course the saw just picked it up and threw it and stove his chest in. He lived for five hours and bled internally.

We got the plane down from Hokitika. It was at the glaciers taking flights, and they had to get a message to the doctor who was on the glaciers. They had to fly back to Hokitika to get his equipment and then fly all the way to Okuru, which took about an hour and ten minutes. The doctor arrived there when dad was just about gone, he was cold. It was fairly tough sort of going for the family, especially after losing my brother.

I milked for a while before I gave it up. There was nothing in homemade butter – we used to have to send it up to a pastry cook in Greymouth. Then I ran a few dry cattle. When I was married we decided to give that up and I took a contract with the Works, driving a truck and I did that for twenty years. When the road was nearly through I got a general licence and carted through to Cromwell. I sold the farm about 1947 and we built a small place at Haast. We lived there for quite some years and then came to Christchurch in about 1973. Prior to that I had sold my trucking business, which wasn't very profitable, and my son and I went crayfishing for fifteen years.

my wife

I met Myra in Christchurch. A friend of my mother's came to Okuru and asked if I would like to go back to Christchurch with her for a holiday, so I did and that's where I met Myra. We arrived at the railway station, and Myra was there to meet her mother. We got engaged after something like three weeks. I went back home and Myra came down on the plane with her brother – it must have been around Christmas time. They stayed for ten days or a fortnight and went back. I went out about April and we were married. We had a few days in Akaroa, then came back to Christchurch and took a railcar to Hokitika, and then flew home to Okuru.

I think Myra had her moments when she didn't like it here, but she settled down remarkably well. We had trips out, not very often, perhaps once a year and Myra might go out for the odd trip but it was too expensive to do often.

No, I didn't think about moving out of the area, not really. There was not much money and not many prospects. You didn't quite know what to do. There came a time when the farm wasn't worth keeping so I sold it to Bill Buchanan and I took the truck that he had and went on the Works. We moved up to Haast and built a small house. Myra's brother helped – or I helped Myra's brother, I should say. He was a carpenter.

Bernie Cowan carrying freight across the soon-to-be-completed bridge at the Gates of Haast, c. 1959. Courtesy of Bernie Cowan

work

Another friend of mine, Ted Buchanan, he had a truck on the Works and we used to do a lot of deer stalking and we had quite a sideline with deerskins. The job was just pure and simple carting gravel. There was men who formed the road and felled the bush. There was hardly a bulldozer on it although they eventually got one. It was just carting gravel from the riverbed. There were days, weeks, years of work just carting gravel. I did bits and pieces on the road right from Haast to Clarke Bluff.

I had a single-axle five-ton truck – they were Fords. Then I had an Austin, the Internationals and then Leylands. I had six trucks at one time but I only actually worked five. We were paid on contract, it was an hourly rate for a start, I forget what it was, about nineteen shillings and sixpence an hour. Then we got what they called a corporative contract, and they paid you by the yard. I think I did about eighteen years with the Public Works and then I did about another two years general carting. Mind you, I was mixing the general carting with the Ministry of Works licence. I did carting through to Cromwell and Alexandra.

My son John had chooks for a while; he had about 2000 birds at Haast. We used to grade the eggs, clean them and sell them locally and take out what couldn't be sold. That only lasted a couple of years and then we found that there was good money in crayfish, so we bought a small boat and away we went.

*Myra Cowan
(née Roberts)
on her
wedding day,
April 1944.*
Courtesy of Myra
Cowan

Chapter 10

'I was just so homesick'

Myra Cowan

Myra (née Roberts) was born in Christchurch in 1921 and was the daughter of a bank officer and a masseuse. She attended St Margaret's College and later worked as a dental assistant in Christchurch. She married Bernie Cowan of Okuru in April 1944. Myra and Bernie had four sons. Murray died in 1956 and Robin drowned in 1984. Myra and Bernie now live in Christchurch.

marrying Bernard

My aunt and mother had known Bernard's mother for many many years. My mother went down to Haast to stay with Mrs Cowan and when she was due to travel home, Bernard travelled with her. I

Myra Cowan (née Roberts), c. 1987.
Courtesy of Myra Cowan

actually met him on the Christchurch Railway Station! Which has always caused a little bit of a laugh.

Our courting was really done with letters. We became engaged before Bernard went back to Haast. We used to write letters every week – there was only a mail service to Haast once a week then. Mine was more or less a diary, I'd write a little bit each night. My brother and I went to Haast for the Christmas before we were married and the sandflies and mosquitoes nearly killed me. I came back to Christchurch in January and we were married in April.

moving to Haast

I was very excited about it. I thought it was going to be a great adventure, which it was. But I was just so homesick, it was dreadful. If anybody looked at me sideways, I'd burst into tears. Finally, I came back home because my brother was going overseas, it was wartime. I came on my own and I was very homesick then for Bernard and I went back to Haast and settled down.

As was done in those days, we were tin-kettled. That was a party to welcome me there. Everybody brought some supper and you usually knew it was going to happen. But the idea was to start off banging tins or anything they could possibly find to announce their arrival. It was rather fun.

I was the outsider. It was very, very lonely at times. I never really felt at ease. I had been down there for quite a long time when the horrible truth leaked out, that I had been to St Margaret's [College] and that was not quite the done thing. I just had to change my ways, which, when looking back, was silly. I asked two of the men to dinner one night and I had serviettes on the table, damask serviettes, I'd always been used to that sort of thing. Apparently that funny little story shot round the district so after that if anyone was coming we didn't use serviettes. I was trying to fit in.

The Cowan houses at Okuru, which became Myra's home in 1944.
Courtesy of Bernie Cowan

my home

We didn't have the conveniences that people have today. To do the washing we would have to boil the copper. No electricity for a long time. So life was fairly busy. We didn't have a lot of time, especially those of us with little children. We were really kept very, very busy but there was always time to stop for a cup of tea or coffee if anyone came in.

I had an old range. I had to learn to stoke and to keep it stoked. One of my big difficulties to begin with was that I'd forget it and it would go out. But it wasn't very long and I could cook with the best of them. We had beautiful firewood – rata, black pine, silver pine for kindling. Beautiful wood which Bernard supplied. I didn't have to chop wood. He saw me one day trying to chop a log of wood and I think he still laughs; he said it was just so pathetic.

[We had] kerosene lamps to begin with. Then we had a very small electric power plant, just enough to run two or three lights. But as time went on we progressed and we had a very good lighting plant [diesel generator]. The first light on would start it and the last light off at night would stop it. Then I could use a jug and a toaster and an electrolux.

I had an electric iron and when Philip, my youngest child, was three months old I got a washing machine. An agitator washing machine which came down by plane. The excitement was great. I remember washing everything that I could lay my hands on, forgetting that it all had to get dry and be ironed. It was very exciting – it made life easier – I didn't have to boil the copper each day.

dances

Usually after the boat came in there would be a dance. The reason for that being that the beer came on the boat. It was mostly beer but then again I am quite sure some of the Ministry of Works employees and the farmers would perhaps have a bottle of whisky or something like that. One of the Nolan boys played the piano and another one played the squeeze box, and if there was anyone visiting who had a musical instrument they would play. They really were great fun but they were country dances. The hall was very old at that time. It could be quite frightening because the floor sloped down to the one and only door, and if you weren't very careful you could slip there. There was an enormous fire-place and the saveloys were heated up on big tins hanging on hooks in the fireplace and we all took plates for supper.

The hall was opposite where we lived. It is no longer there; it has been gone for a long time. Some came by horseback, some came by boat from Jackson Bay – I suppose sometimes there were forty or fifty people. Mostly the beer was drunk that night, there could be some left over which was consumed on the Sunday morning – or I should say later on Sunday morning – the dances used to go till very late. It wasn't a very successful dance if we went home before daylight.

The Whitebaiters' Ball was the social event of the year. People came from long distances away. This traveller would arrive with his caravan with lots of pretty dresses and would try to sell them to us because the Whitebaiters' Ball was really a dress-up occasion. Before that we would perhaps order clothes from Hokitika, write a letter to Addisons which was *the* beautiful shop in Hokitika. We'd give them sizes and ideas of what we wanted and they were quite terrific. They would send down a box to me of four or five or six frocks that they thought might suit me to wear to the ball. A little bit of eyeing went on, to see who had the best dress.

my children

My first two babies were born here [Christchurch] and my other two babies were born in Greymouth. We always talked about coming out from Haast or going in. I came out quite early to see a doctor

A social gathering or perhaps the morning after? This photo was probably taken in the late 1930s. Bernie Cowan is fourth from the left. Courtesy of Bernie Cowan

and to be booked in, and then a month before my babies were due I would have to go. I took John home when he was four weeks old. Travelled in the rail car at two o'clock in the morning from Christchurch over to Hokitika. My dad went with me. And then flew down in the plane to Haast.

I used to be very anxious at times. I was fortunate, the babies were healthy and did what they were supposed to do. Until John was about eighteen months, my sister-in-law still lived beside me and she had children, so she was helpful. But when things went wrong it was a terrible worry to me because I was not a West Coaster. I was a city girl – we'd always had a doctor on call any time he was wanted and I did find that very worrying.

Murray died of cancer when he was seven. By this time the plane was down every week or more. We had noticed that he had a swelling on his left wrist. We used to have a monthly visit from a doctor, who came by plane, and she had a look at it and wanted us to take him to Greymouth and have it X-rayed. That was the beginning of a nightmare. We had no idea that there was anything wrong. He had a tumour on the bone in his wrist. After three months his left arm was amputated and we had him for fourteen months after that when he died of cancer of the lungs. One little cell got away. [He came home after his arm was amputated] and he went to school and the children were absolutely wonderful with him. They accepted him as the little boy that he'd always been, they didn't make big fusses but they were very careful and gentle with him.

When I was bringing up my family, it was a very free life. There was very little traffic, there was wide open spaces, and there was the bush. It really was a wonderful place to bring up children because there were not the stresses and the strains that there are today. In the Haast township there were quite a lot of children, and they would play their games together and build their huts and have a lovely time.

Residents of Haast and Okuru at Haast in 1949. Myra and children are second from the right.
Courtesy of Des Nolan

Ancestors of Betty Eggeling née Buchanan

William BUCHANAN
Born: 1877 in Sydney, Australia
Married: c. 1916 in Runanga, Westland
Died: February 1940 in Hokitika, Westland

Milcah Elizabeth (Betty) BUCHANAN
Born: 1920 in Ross, Westland

Martha Isabella (Bella) JONES
Born: 1897 in Victoria, Australia
Died: March 1983 in Greymouth, Westland

The Buchanan children at Ikamatua, c. 1930. From left: Ted, Myra, Bruce, Betty, Bill and Henry. Dandy, the horse, was brought down to Okuru when the family moved there from Ikamatua.
Courtesy of Betty Eggeling

Chapter 11

'We were so thrilled to have running water'

Betty Eggeling

Betty (née Buchanan) was born in Ross in 1920, and moved with her family to Okuru in the early 1930s. Before her marriage to Charlie Eggeling, Betty was a housekeeper further up the coast at Karangarua and spent two years psychiatric nursing at Seaview Hospital, Hokitika. Betty and Charlie spent an enjoyable retirement exploring the Haast district. Charlie passed away in 1995 having reached the grand age of ninety-seven. Betty is still living at the Turnbull, next door to one of her sons and his family, and is still keen on the outdoor life. I frequently found Betty about to go out on a mission in her four-wheeler.

my parents

My father was born in Sydney. He was educated as an accountant but not liking being closed in, only stuck at it for twelve months then took off to the Victorian goldfields. At the age of twenty-three, he decided to try his luck in New Zealand.

Betty Eggeling (née Buchanan) at her whitebait stand, October 1997.
Courtesy of Betty Eggeling

My mother's father came out from Wales to Australia and married there. My mother was the eldest daughter and left Australia at the age of seven. They shifted around a lot on first arriving in New Zealand, finally they brought a dairy farm in Otumoetai, that's just out of Tauranga. At the age of sixteen my mother came down to Greymouth to work and it was there that she married my father. Her mother's sister had married Dad and when the second child was born, she died. Mum came down to look after her uncle by marriage and his two children. They later married.

Dad was a coal miner in Runanga at that time. My second brother [Bill] was born in Aratika, where Dad was working on the railway. I'm the third child and I was born in Ross. Dad went tram-laying for the mill until the Ross water-supply dam burst one stormy night and washed our house off its foundations. We shifted away from Ross to a farm on the south side of Rough River at Ikamatua. Mum milked cows, raised kids and grew potatoes to feed the family over the depression years. Dad went away tram-laying and came home on weekends.

It was in Ikamatua that my sister [Myra] was born. We were fed and put to bed early on this very wet night. Then we heard a horse and gig arrive. We kids knew that something was going on but it wasn't until morning that we heard that a new baby was there.

We always did have enough to eat, thanks to Mum. She toiled so hard for us. There were times when she didn't even have any flour. She reared pigs and she killed them and made her own bacon. We lived on bacon and potatoes that she grew. She always seemed to manage to get beef shins and she used to feed us on a lot of soup. She grew marvellous rhubarb, and we ate a lot of rhubarb. Mum used to carry all the water from Rough River, she used to carry it up quite a steep cliff. There was just a cattle track down and she used to walk up this track. I really don't know how she survived.

We had very little clothing. I remember her making boys' pants. I think different people must have given her old skirts and that sort of thing, and she would make these pants for the boys and she would line them with flour bags, the old linen flour bags they used to have. When I went to school, I went in flour-bag frocks and she used to have a wee bit of floral material around the sleeves and the neck. I didn't put shoes on my feet until I was eleven, just because we couldn't afford it.

When I was ten, mother decided to send me up to Otumoetai, to my grandparents, as she was having such a struggle keeping us fed. I went up in early December and was to stay indefinitely, but I hated it. Grandad practically ignored me and Granny used to give me things to eat while he wasn't looking. I was sent back to Ikamatua only weeks before we left there to come down here to Okuru.

moving to Okuru

Dad had come down on several two-monthly trips previously. He came down with a friend, Norm Wallis, who had taken up a lot of timber in the area and wanted Dad to tram-lay for bringing timber into a mill which wasn't yet built. While he was here, Dad bought a farm off the Cuttances who were preparing to trek off over the Haast Pass with their horses, cattle dogs and even their fowls.

Our gear had to be loaded on a dray to be shipped to the railway station at Ikamatua, to go to Hokitika, to catch the boat. We had one horse, three pigs, nine cows, hens and ducks aboard. It was very hard work for Mum. Mum sort of more or less did as Dad told her. I don't know whether they discussed it. I know that when Mum got here it was a big struggle, but she did shift into much better accommodation. We were so thrilled to have running water and a stove to cook on, which we never had up there.

At about midday we chugged out over a fairly rough Hokitika Bar. We headed into a fairly stiff sou'west sea which made our horse and pigs quite seasick. After about thirty hours at sea, and waiting out at Open Bay Islands for the tide to rise enough, we went in over the bar of the Okuru River. We made our landing on 19 May 1931. Father was here all along, Mum did it all.

home life

We lived on pigeons, ducks, eels, fish and black swans as well. We had no meat of our own to kill at that time, but when money allowed we would buy half a sheep off other farmers such as the Harrises or Eggelings, as they lived on the Turnbull, too.

We had thirteen cows we milked through the summer. Mum separated the milk through a separator and made butter. She used to wash the buttermilk out of it very thoroughly, salt it heavily and pack it in bulk to be shipped up to Greymouth on the next trip of the *Gael*. She used to get thruppence a pound. She learnt it through necessity. It's Mum that's the amazing person. It's not the ones that have followed on, it's her. The ones that have followed on have had it easy.

Flour was always our biggest item in the stores when they arrived. Sometimes, if it was too long between boats, it would get damp. At times the weevils would attack it so it all had to be sifted. One time when the bar shoaled up, which it often did in the winter, the district ran out of flour.

I don't think she told us off much at all. She used to try and keep a bit of law and order, but I think she was too busy. You know, after she'd done a day's work, she would come in and cook a meal for us and I can't remember ever putting myself out to help her. Kids do it all the time, and I think I was just as bad. She used to get us to pick up potatoes and we

wouldn't do it, we'd fight and throw potatoes at each other and here was Mum trying to get it all done.

Oh yes, we did [help with chores] but like all kids we had to be hounded into it. One of the big chores we always had to do was pump the water. Each one of us had to do so much on the pump until the tank flowed over. That was almost an everyday thing and we always had to milk the cows. We used to hand milk and then we used to have to turn the separator. We used to help, although I don't ever remember doing very much housework and I didn't do a great deal of cooking either.

Dad did work a bit on the farm, putting in fences and things like that. Henry and Bill and Bruce used to help him. He was tram-laying over the Okuru, he had huts over there and he would be in the hut and possibly come home each weekend. I can't really remember whether he did

The house on the Turnbull River that the Buchanan family moved into in 1931.

much work around the farm when he came home on weekends. I never ever remember him in the cowshed or anything like that. If he did anything it would be mending fences and those sorts of jobs. He never ploughed or anything. Mum did all that.

He was very like Henry. He used to round us up quite often but then I suppose we deserved it. I used to be called Milcah until I came and said to the family I want that name changed – I want to take Betty, which is Elizabeth. Dad used to always call me Betsy. When I was in the wrong, and I was going to get a hiding, it was always Milcah.

farming

Our farm was only a small one. As time went on we bought McPhersons' and we bought in some of the old Harris paddocks, when Joe and George sold out to their nephews, Tom and Bill. Then we bought Cowans' farm as well, so we only started off little but we grew as time went on.

The Harrises were always good friends with the Buchanans and as a teenage girl I went with them often, mustering the valleys. The Okuru and Turnbull valleys were theirs at that time. Farming down here is very fragmented, it was just as areas came up for sale, which means each farmer's paddocks are scattered here and there and it's still like that.

I've always enjoyed mustering and riding horses. I drove through the cattle track with Charlie at times. I used to enjoy it, loved it. Especially if you got a dry trip. One time we got snow between Fox and Franz and I got so cold that when I arrived at Charlie's cousin's place, where we always stayed, I went straight to bed. I went after I had one, two and three children. By the time I had the fourth, fifth and sixth the cattle droving might have been over.

Before the event of the helicopter shooting of the deer, it was usual to look out from the Clarke Bluff up the Landsborough and see mobs of three and four hundred at evening time. You would see many along the roadside wherever you went. They got so plentiful that they were coming down the rivers into our front paddocks. Of course, they were eating themselves out of food, and because of that you would not get the lovely big antlers that you did previously.

They were like the rabbits to us. We didn't have rabbits but we had deer. The mobs of deer got so bad that our cattle, that we put out to winter on the river runs, were dying of starvation. We lost a lot of cattle and we couldn't use the runs. When Graham Stewart started helicopter shooting, it wasn't unusual for them to shoot five hundred deer at a time on the slopes on top of the mountains.

communication

For many many years we had a single telephone wire running alongside the cattle track. We could send telegrams or communicate with Hokitika but the message would have to be relayed several times. We could ring each other within the district but there would be many more that you would be speaking to than the one you rang. Especially one lady, who was a heavy breather. In bad weather the wire would get pulled down or broken and then we were isolated. With the second settlement of Jackson Bay [1937] we got a post office and weather station down there, so all our communications went to Awarua by radio. A lot of our medical messages, accidents and that sort of thing, went through to Awarua.

Up to a couple of years before the Harris nephews sold the farm there was only the dray road up the north side of the Turnbull River, the homestead being on the south side. The river had to be forded all the time either in the dray or on horseback. The two nephews' wives were both Wellingtonians and not used to such isolation. There was no access at all in flood times. It was one of those girls who was pregnant and came into labour seven weeks early. We had a sea fog down at sea level and an emergency aircraft could not get down. A little boy was born at the district nurse's cottage. For three whole days the fog did not lift. The nurse kept pots boiling on the wood stove to assist the wee mite's breathing. She lost the battle on the evening of the second day. I was her assistant and I baptised him before he was taken. He now lies in Okuru cemetery beside his grandmother.

my husband

I really don't know how Charlie and I first met. When I was that age I had no cobbers or anything, there was nobody here. I used to go out riding a lot on my own, just riding the bush tracks round. Perhaps we met that way.

We got married in Greymouth. It was during the war and we were hoping to go up to the Bay of Islands [for our honeymoon]. Somehow or other, whether the trains didn't run or something, we couldn't get away anyway so we more or less didn't have a honeymoon. It was something to do with the war.

Dick [Charlie's brother] stayed here with us. He stayed with us for practically all our married life which was a disaster. We never fought and he was good and all that, but he was just always there. I wouldn't do it again.

my children

I used to go out [when the baby was due] in the Fox Moth and that had little sack seats and the bar came across under your legs and it wasn't very comfortable. It took about an hour-ten to about an hour-and-a-half to get from Haast to Hokitika. For a start I went out about a month before but as time went on I got more experienced. I used to know almost to the fortnight and I used to go out sometimes just a week ahead. You get to know if you have enough. I would come back in practically straight away but we were in hospital a fortnight in those days, we weren't

Betty's pram for her first-born, Peter, c. 1943. Courtesy of Betty Eggeling

just thrown out like they are now. The baby would be about three weeks old when we brought it home. Yes, we'd fly home again. When the baby was on the plane the pilots always kept low.

I think mostly Mum did [look after the other children], then I had different friends that would take an older one. That's what we did. I took a lot of other people's children too, as well as them taking mine. It was [neighbourly] until the road came through and then people all went their own ways. When we just had the boat coming, we used to share out provisions until they were all gone and that sort of thing. Yes, it was so different in here on our own.

entertainment

Every time the boat came in, the *Gael*, it would be loaded and every time we would have a dance that night – of course there was plenty of drink there. They never got out of hand, they never drank to the extent of being obnoxious and that sort of thing. They were great evenings, those dance evenings and, of course, the drink never came into the hall. You wouldn't see a lady drinking.

The piano accordion or a violin [provided the music], just whatever anybody could play – a piano, you know, whatever. It wasn't always good music but still there was nothing better and it was enjoyable. Mum let me go quite early but the biggest punishment she could ever give me was to stop me going to a dance. Oh, that was awful, and she did a few times too. My brother Bill used to take me and I used to enjoy them. At the dances was another place that I met Charlie. He was quite a good dancer and he more or less used to teach me to dance. I was going with Charlie before I left school, and yet I think of it now – if a thing like that happened now, in our generation, we'd be calling that person a dirty old man because I was so young. But it was absolutely nothing like that, he was so trustworthy really. I wouldn't like my daughter to, but you didn't think of those things in those days.

starting the motor camp

Well, when the road opened from Otago so many people would come in and then it would rain or they'd stayed too late and they couldn't get back because it was rough in those days and they'd come in and ask for accommodation. The carpenter that built Bruce's and Ted's [Betty's brothers] places was here then and he built himself a hut to use while he was doing that job. He went up back to Picton and said, 'If you send my gear up to me, I will give you that hut.' So that's what I did. The hut was still out in the paddock there, so we shifted it out by the road and I let it for a start. Then from there we put in the ablution block and built a couple of cabins and from then on all we made out of it we put back into it. Then it grew and grew.

Of course in those days we had no power. We had the diesel motor, and you know how people go crook with a diesel. We had it right up here in the corner but even so they used to growl, and I put it off at about half-past ten too. I also had the big diesel burners for the water, but they used to soot up something awful and all the soot would come out over the tents. Greasy soot. They used to go crook and I don't blame them, it was just awful. But it was the best we could do.

We had it for eighteen or twenty years and then it got too much for us. We were older and I felt that it needed younger people. We didn't want to employ anyone, we were doing it ourselves, I was milking cows at that time and looking after the kids and all that sort of thing. And anyway we sold it and it was after that then that we were free to go down the beach.

Kerry (my son) found a nice piece of greenstone on the beach many years before and we always said that when we sold the motor-camp we would go and look and see what's down there [in the Cascade

Betty and Charlie Eggeling at the Jackson Bay Centennial Celebrations, 1976. Courtesy of Betty Eggeling

area]. So that's what we did. We spent a lot of time down there. We used to go down to the mouth of the Cascade and stay in the whitebaiters' huts and go from there. Oh it was lovely – it was the best part of our lives, I think.

Mary (née Clifford) and William Harris. Courtesy of Mary Jones

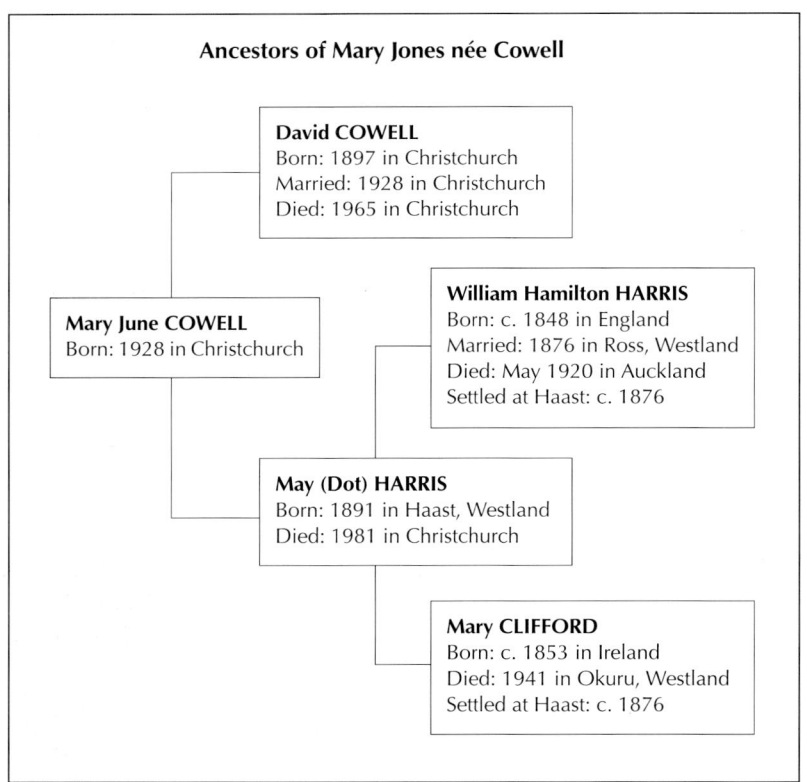

Ancestors of Mary Jones née Cowell

David COWELL
Born: 1897 in Christchurch
Married: 1928 in Christchurch
Died: 1965 in Christchurch

Mary June COWELL
Born: 1928 in Christchurch

William Hamilton HARRIS
Born: c. 1848 in England
Married: 1876 in Ross, Westland
Died: May 1920 in Auckland
Settled at Haast: c. 1876

May (Dot) HARRIS
Born: 1891 in Haast, Westland
Died: 1981 in Christchurch

Mary CLIFFORD
Born: c. 1853 in Ireland
Died: 1941 in Okuru, Westland
Settled at Haast: c. 1876

Chapter 12

'I was a terrible tomboy'

Mary Jones

Mary (née Cowell) was born in Christchurch in 1928 and moved to Huhuka on the Turnbull River in about 1932. She absolutely loved growing up on the farm and spoke of her childhood in glowing terms. After her family moved away in 1944, Mary finished her schooling in Christchurch and then worked as a clerk and secretary. She married Brian Jones in 1965 and had two children. Mary retained her love of everything outdoors and was also interested in sports, music and gardening. She passed away in 1998.

my grandparents

My grandmother, who was Mary Clifford, came out from Ireland. She came out during the potato famine and went to stay with her uncle. That was during the gold rush and she worked as a housemaid for my uncle and aunt for quite a long time, and then she went down to Gillespies Beach. We always thought she was a housemaid down there, until recently we found her marriage certificate and it said that she was a barmaid! That was something we never ever knew of, granny being a barmaid. It was there that she met grandad and married him. Now Grandad came from Middlesex and he was brought up by a very strict Presbyterian family – I think it was

Mary Jones (née Cowell) with her family in Christchurch.
Courtesy of Brian Jones

131

an auntie; what happened to his parents we really don't know. Grandad was very restricted at home, he wasn't allowed to whistle or do anything on a Sunday and he got a bit fed-up with that and ran away to sea. He found his way to Hokitika and eventually Gillespies, where Grandma was. When they went to South Westland I am not too sure, but they moved to just south of Haast. The trees are still there on the Haast Beach.

My grandfather set up a store there and used to supply people with tinned food and things like that. He had the farm and an orchard. They were there for many years. The children were all educated at the Haast School which was about half a mile or a mile down the road towards the Haast River. As the older members of the Harris family grew up, the girls taught the younger ones, but they did have a school teacher. His name was Mr Scully.

My eldest uncle, his name was Noah Harris and he was born in a very big flood. Grandma was expecting this baby and Mrs Cron from further up the road, up by what is now the Haast Bridge, she was to come down and help deliver the baby. Grandma went into labour and Grandad was going to go up and get Mrs Cron and he couldn't get, because of this huge flood, and he had to deliver the baby himself. The baby had been born and Grandad looked out the door. Everything was surrounded by water, so they called the baby Noah.

At some stage the family moved up the Turnbull River, about five miles inland from Okuru. They set up the farm as I knew it and the homestead there. Mum was quite a young girl when she first went up there to cook for them, she thinks she was about twelve or thirteen. She

The Harris family house at Huhuka. Mary and William Harris with some of their children, c. 1909. Courtesy of Mary Jones

The Huhuka Homestead, Upper Okuru, c. 1909. Courtesy of Mary Jones

used to go up and cook the meals while they were away mustering the cattle. Her earliest memories of being up there were going out at night and she would listen for the men coming back. She could hear the dogs and the men shouting, but the main thing she remembered was all the bird life about there. Kakapo, weka, bitterns, you know, the boom boom of them. There were all these birds that are not about today. They were her earliest recollections of Huhuka, as our place was called.

Over the years the whole family shifted there but a lot of the family had grown up because you've got a big gap between the eldest and the youngest with eleven. The girls went away to work. Noah and Jim married two Cuttance girls from there and they shifted away. There were two boys left on the farm and a sister who never married and they were George, Joe and Lil. They ended up living on the farm with Grandma.

Grandpa died in 1926. He had rheumatism and he went up to Auckland and Rotorua for the waters and then died of a heart attack. Grandma didn't die until the 1940s, so there was a long time that she was a widow. She was a very upright lady, very regal. It's only after she died – there's a couple of letters about here, and when I read the letters I realised how Irish she was.

my parents

My mother was Dot. She worked here in Christchurch and also in Wellington. It was in Christchurch that she met and married my father and they lived there during the depression. I was born in 1928 and my brother in 1931. After my brother was born he got whooping cough and was quite sick with it. Mum had had a trip home before I was born but hadn't been back since. The doctor said, what your son needs is some good country air. In those days Dad couldn't get work and things were pretty desperate. I think they lived on bread and water, just about, trying to keep us kids.

moving to Haast

Mum decided to go over and see Grandma and that's how we came to live in South Westland. We went down from Paringa by horse. That was the only way in; it was very rough. I would be three and I left there when I was sixteen. When we got down there Mum and Dad milked cows on the farm for quite a long time and made butter. I used to milk the cows too. I loved the cattle and had pet cows and calves and used to ride the calves and everything. I was a real tomboy. I used to disappear when the pigs were killed. I didn't mind eating the beautiful bacon, but I didn't like seeing them killed.

Round about that time they started the road that was going to connect Hokitika to Okuru. They did the stretch from Haast to Jackson Bay and that's where Dad worked first. After some time they gave Dad the job of painting and renovating all the buildings at Jackson Bay. So, anyway, we stayed on the farm and Dad lived in single quarters at the Public Works and he would come home every week or perhaps every two or three weeks. Both David and I grew up on the farm and we did correspondence school because we were five miles from the school. We had a river between us and the school and that could be too high to cross, it didn't take much rain really.

Mary and her brother David doing schoolwork at Huhuka.
Courtesy of Mary Jones

I went right through to the fifth form with correspondence and then when I came to Christchurch at the age of sixteen I did two years at St Mary's. Our lessons used to come every fortnight and Mum would supervise us. I took a commercial course in high school, and I did shorthand and typing. Normally they would have sent you a typewriter to practise on but because of the war it didn't happen. With the shorthand, Mum used to dictate to me; it was pretty demanding for her.

growing up on the farm

I grew up with a great love of the farm. I loved all the animals. There is a story going that when I was a bit smaller and grizzling and growling about going to bed, Mum said 'All right, get your pyjamas and go and sleep with the calves.' And that is what I did. Dad had to go and retrieve me from down the road. I had no fear of the dark or anything. I used to roam the farm and the bush. It's a wonder I didn't get lost or killed or something when I think about it. I used to cross the river when it was very low. Mum would have had a fit if she had known that.

I used to work to a timetable with my correspondence school [lessons]. If you didn't, you'd get behind. I would perhaps do longer hours, or do some of it in the evenings, and then I would be allowed to go mustering with my uncles. I could ride a horse, of course. I had my own sort of fancy horse. I would go away for a day with them, mustering the cattle. They kept sheep on the Haast Beach. They'd bring them down to the Okuru River, and then they'd have to be enticed to swim that and come up five miles inland to be shorn. If you have ever had anything to do with sheep, trying to get them in the water is another thing.

I was always getting into trouble with pet lambs. One got into the garden one time and went along nipping all of Mum's asters. I had a pet possum that was brought in because we didn't have possums down there then. He eventually got killed by a dog, I think. I had cats and kittens, and Dad was always drowning the kittens. I was quite at peace with those sorts of things, they were just things that were natural. Killing sheep for meat for the house, I would stand there and see a sheep have its throat cut; those things were things that happened. I used to love to skin the sheep. So I was a real farm girl. I was mad on dogs. I took all Mum's tablecloths and put them in the kennel with Nellie and her puppies.

our home

The house was a four-roomed house and one of them was used as a living room so there were three rooms for bedrooms. It was made from pit-sawn timber. As a girl [I remember] the pit still up in the

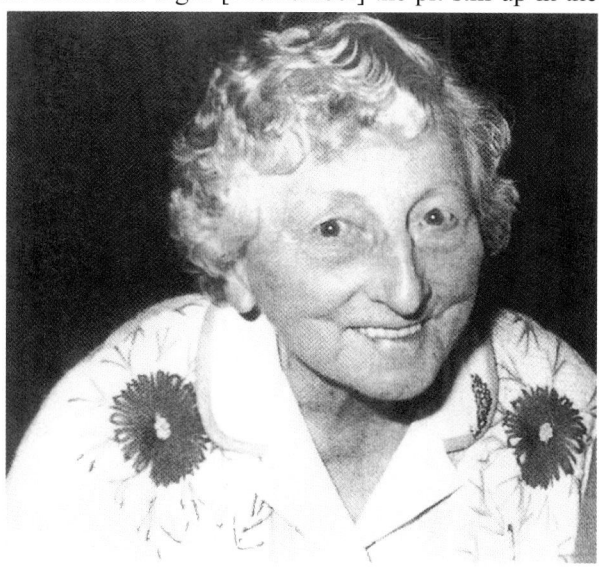

Dot Cowell (née Harris), Mary's mother, at the Jackson Bay Centennial Celebrations, 1976.
Courtesy of Myra Fulton

bush. Of course, it was all bush when the family went up there so they had to mill all the timber, cut it down and make it into paddocks. It was all cut and then burnt and then grass grown.

The house at Huhuka [became] T-shaped. The T that was put on was a living room and a kitchen. They were big rooms with high ceilings, lino on the floor and mats. In the kitchen there was a big family table, [and] a wood stove with a double oven. In one corner was a sink and a small bench. At one end there was a beautiful stag's antlers, a twenty-four-pointer I think, and on that hung the rifles. We had a shotgun, a .22, and Joe and George both had their .303s.

We knew we didn't touch them because they were something that killed. Never thought about it. I used to stand by my uncles when they cleaned them and oiled them, I knew all about that. It was just something that came naturally. Mum was a good shot. I tell you what, in today's world you'd be in trouble, but my mother could shoot a pigeon no trouble at all. They made lovely stew – though, of course, if you were caught with pigeon you were fined. It was £500 so that was a lot of money. The pigeons used to come down on the fruit when it was ripening.

I always remember, we had a very distinguished person here from the government, he'd come to see about the Governor-General's *aide-de-camp* coming to do some deer shooting on my uncle's property. We were all sitting in the lounge talking, all niceties, etc. and Grandma looked out the window, and there's a couple of jolly pigeons in her plum tree and she just said, 'Those dang pigeons, I must get George to shoot them.' There was this deadly silence.

Breakfast would consist of porridge, always, and fresh cream of course, and sugar or golden syrup or whatever you liked. Bacon and eggs usually, because the men were doing manual work. When you got up in the morning you had to light the range to cook anything. Lunch was the main meal of the day, you would have either roast mutton or boiled mutton, ditto, ditto, ditto and at nights you would have cold meats and perhaps the vegies that were left over. Puddings, well there was tapioca, rice, bread-and-butter pudding – all of those I hated. There was fruit; Grandma used to bottle fruit of course, preserves and jam and stuff like that. And there were cakes, buns and biscuits because they always baked.

Christmas Day for our main meal we always had a goose. Grandma had geese and ducks and hens. The other thing I remember is jelly and whipped cream. It was the same as in town I suppose, same as now. It was a special time for everyone to be together. But being so far, only now and again would the other members of Gran's family come to see her, mostly the girls. It was a big event for any of them to come and see Grandma and they would stay for probably a month. You see, the only transport in and out was the boat and then Captain Mercer started up his air service.

When the air service was set up, I was nearly six.

That's my earliest recollections of Christmas and Father Christmas. I always thought he came by plane. I had heaps of dolls because my aunts all sent dolls and didn't realise I was growing up.

clothing

Mum said that each Christmas Grandma would buy a new dress, and the eldest girl got that dress and her dress was passed down, so the youngest one got the one that was well-worn. In my time my mother made my own clothes. She would get samples from Addisons in Hokitika, and she would pick out the materials. We just wore dresses. We didn't wear trousers or anything like that. Even riding, we used to wear dresses. When I was older, fourteen or fifteen, I made myself a trouser suit with Mum's help. Those were the first trousers that I wore. I only wore those when I went riding on horses, you know, when I went down to Okuru to get the mail or something. My mother used to wear my uncle's dungaree trousers if she went riding on the farm, because you know skirts are a bit hard to ride in really, even though they were full skirts.

my uncles and aunt

Lil was unmarried and she just worked on the farm until the farm was sold and then she came to live in Christchurch. A biggish woman, a lady who had a pretty short temper, she used to get very huffy over things and when she got huffy she went to bed. She was the one that stayed home. In those days there always seemed to be somebody who stayed home and never married or never went away to work. She was a bit different from the rest of them, the rest were all bright and happy and she really didn't have that sense of humour that the others had. So, whether Grandma thought she might not manage in the world, I don't know. But there was always a girl that stayed home and she perhaps never wanted to shift.

And my two uncles; one was a very placid man, George. The other one, Joe, could be a bit more fiery. But they were both wonderful, they were like a father to me really. Hard-working men, very

Joe Harris at Huhuka. Courtesy of Mary Jones.

George Harris at Huhuka.
Courtesy of Mary Jones

hard-working men. It was only in very later life that Joe ended up marrying Bella Buchanan – her family was all grown up. Of course Mr Buchanan, Bill Bucas we used to call him, he had died. I remember when he died. I was always a bit frightened of him – he always seemed a very gruff man.

air service

I was his [Bert Mercer's] first patient. I would be about six and I got all these symptoms of appendicitis. There was a big

The convenience of airmail! Din Nolan hands the mailbag to Bert Mercer.
Courtesy of Des Nolan

northerly storm coming in which meant flooding. It was September and Mum rang the district nurse at Te Taho, which is up near Whataroa. She said, 'That's appendicitis. You will have to get her out.' Mum said, 'I don't think I'm going to get her out.' Well, to cut a long story short, I was eventually transported by boat across the Turnbull River. Dinny Nolan came round and picked me up in his horse and gig and I was taken down to their place and Captain Mercer came in and picked me up. He was over here in Christchurch and he had to go to Hokitika and pick someone up there and then fly down and pick me up and get me back to Hokitika. I was operated on about an hour after I got in there and they reckoned I only had about two hours before I would have got peritonitis. When the air service went in there, that was an absolute godsend. About a fortnight later, Des Nolan's father was taken out and then Des, both with appendicitis. They used to die there you know. Mrs Eggeling was one. Mum looked after her. Sickness down there was a traumatic thing. They could be taken out overland but it meant taking you on a stretcher and it was many miles.

Captain Mercer decided to set up a service down to South Westland because there was nothing like it about and he had this Fox Moth. Of course we had no aerodrome down there – so the Nolans, they had a paddock in front of their house which they levelled off and he used that. Then we had another one set up at Mussel Point. The next landing point was Arawata. They didn't do much, you know, they just levelled a paddock off. He ran a service once a week or, if there was quite a bit of stuff to be brought down, it was twice a week. He was a very nice man. He ended up being killed when he was a passenger in a plane, which was rather traumatic. He made a wonderful difference to South Westland – it was just incredible. The people of South Westland just thought he was wonderful.

learning to ride

I used to be taken on a horse on front of my uncles. They used to have a couple of sacks rolled up strapped to the saddle, I used to go in front or behind. I started when I arrived there, when I was three, and then you just progressed. I used to ride the cows, the calves, anything like that, get dumped off them and everything. I grew up riding horses, barebacked, saddled, whatever.

Bella Buchanan

Mrs Buchanan was wonderful. She had a hard life. She had no carpet or lino or anything on the floor because her place used to get flooded. She lived by a creek and she had the creek one side and the river the other. If you had a big flood, the water came into her place a foot or two feet deep. So, she needed to be able to sweep it out. I always remember there was only bare boards in that house. We always used to call into her place for a cup of tea. She just loved to see someone and as kids we used to go down and stay a night there or something like that. We'd help milk the cows. She had cows, that was her living, milking cows, and she'd have butter and stuff which she sold and her cattle which she sold. But she worked very hard and she had quite a big family.

She made a good job of bringing them up. She used to say, 'Ah, he's a disaster' or 'She's a disaster' or something like that. There must have been bad days when, like all kids do, they rebelled. She might have wanted help with the garden or whatever. She had her own garden but every now and again, especially in the spring, the floods would go through and sweep everything before them and she had to clean it all out again. I always remember being at her place for a cup of tea. I used to bring her mail up to her if I was down there, and you always had a cup of tea. We would have bread, it always seemed to be fresh, and butter, raspberry jam or plum jam or whatever, whipped cream on top of it. They should have all died of heart disease, and I don't think any of them have.

She lived a very simple life. They had simple food

because she could not afford to buy it. She was very poor. Another thing I remember about her place was the daffodils. She had them everywhere around her place – they were beautiful. She used to get me a big bunch to take home. Another thing I remember about her was that she had a bed quilt made out of possum skins. She'd brought that from north because we didn't have possums down there.

Ted, he's the youngest of that family, he's older than I am. He and I used to wrestle. I was a terrible tomboy. We used to have some real wrestling matches, we used to both get hurt. I used to sometimes get the better of him and sometimes it would be the other way around, but if I got the better of him in the wrestling match he used to get that tart. Can you imagine – brothers saying, 'A girl beat you!'

whitebait

Something I do remember about the whitebait was seeing it coming up in a big black ribbon up the river, and cans of whitebait sitting on the side of the road waiting for Nolans to pick it up. Mrs Buchanan used to whitebait the Turnbull River and when the whitebait was running she wouldn't be able to keep pace with the tins – a big black ribbon. People would eat anything else but whitebait. We got sick of it. People used to put it in their gardens for fertiliser – and feed the chooks – and it just sounds dreadful today, doesn't it?

Mary Jones returns to Huhuka, c. 1990.
Courtesy of Brian Jones

floods

If you got a very big northerly in the spring time, it melted the snow and in a very short time you would have a raging flood. I can remember once or twice a very big flood which really flooded all our paddocks, and you knew that the people at Okuru, and especially Mrs Buchanan, were in real trouble, that they would have a very high flood around them. It must have been very daunting to have a couple of feet of water in your house, and look out and all you can see is water.

You knew all the signs and I can see my uncles now, standing at the lounge door with a pair of binoculars and they would get a fix on the river which you could see out across the paddocks. They would have a look in another half hour and if it was rising they would know that there was a big flood coming and they would go and round all the sheep off the flats and bring them into the home paddocks. Sometimes it was a race against time and the water would be coming through. It's amazing how quickly the rivers can rise over there.

There would be heaps of water around and that would all back up over the paddocks just out in front of us, and with that would come the eels. Lots of eels, slimy looking things. Sometimes we would go out and catch them, and they'd be cooked up and given to the dogs. We had about a dozen or sixteen dogs, you know, cattle dogs and so forth. There was an incident one time which was absolutely hilarious. Aunt Lil decided that she would cook these eels that we had caught in this flood. She put them in a kerosene tin. Eels are pretty hard to kill, they take a long time to die no matter whether you whack them on the tail or the head or chop their heads off. But anyway, to all intents and purposes they were dead, so she brought the kerosene tin into the wash house, where the hot water was, and poured the hot water on and of course brought the eels to life. There was eels slithering everywhere and Aunty Lil crying out for help. They were big eels too.

weasels

Nana had a couple of dozen chooks and a couple of roosters, same with the ducks and the geese. We used to have a bit of trouble with weasels and of course they are devastating. All they do is kill something, suck a bit of a blood and go to the next one. Several times the hen house was decimated by weasels. This weasel arrived in the daylight and Grandma called out to George and said, 'George, there's a weasel over there, get your gun.' So George got the shot-gun and he went out and fired a shot at the weasel, which was sitting up on something on the hen house. The hen house was made of corrugated iron and what happened was the shot hit the iron and ricocheted back. How he didn't get hit with it I don't know, but it came through the kitchen window, missed Granny who had just walked away, but it left these holes in the window. So that was an interesting lesson. They got the weasel!

going to high school

Oh, difficult! I had been used to being, you might say, my own boss. I had learnt to work on my own, at my own pace. I had a lot of work to do, at secondary school you do, you are timetabled the same as children in town. But I found it very difficult sitting in class listening and looking at the blackboard and then, when I went home, doing all the homework. To me that was like a double day of school because I was used to spending five hours and the rest of the time was my own. I found it difficult taking it in. I think my concentration span was quite short because I had never had to listen like that.

All the girls there got the wrong idea – they thought I came from Australia. The other thing I had trouble with was sports. I had to learn to play sports. Netball was no bother but tennis, even today I absolutely hate tennis. The older girls would try and teach me tennis and I had no co-ordination or anything. I had no idea how to use a tennis racquet. Those are the things you miss out on when you live in an isolated area like we did. I never learnt to play sports at all until I came to Christchurch as a sixteen-year-old. Apart from netball, I also took up cross-country running which I found very fulfilling.

leaving

I think we moved for work for me and my brother. There was nothing down there for us to do. There was only farming. As far as office work went, there was nothing. I suppose there was the Ministry of Works and I suppose they had an office but it was usually men in those places. There was nothing else for us, especially for girls. A boy could work on a farm, or go and work for Ministry of Works or Rope Construction when they were building the bridges. But other than that, there was nothing.

We came out by air and just brought out our clothes. We didn't have any furniture or anything, so it was only suitcases and ourselves. It was a mixture of excitement of coming to the city, but also leaving the farm. Coming to the city I felt pretty closed in. My aunt Lil Cowell was a wonderful aunt to me. I had been here a few months, and she said she would help get me into a tramping club.

When I look back, I think how primitive we probably were down there compared with some other parts of the West Coast, but there are parts of New Zealand that are still pretty isolated. We didn't know about things so we didn't miss them. Yes, I do think it was a good place to grow up. Those of us who grew up down there and have come out to, you might say, civilisation, have done well for themselves. I enjoyed my life on the farm – it was wonderful, it was free. It was easy and there was no troubles.

Notes

Chapter 1

1 Paul Madgwick, *Aotea: A History of the South Westland Maori*, Printed by Greymouth Evening Star, 1992, p. 24. Mike Rochford, *The Kati Waewae Myth*, 1993, p. 3.

2 Herries Beattie, 'Traditions and Legends collected from the natives of Murihiku', *Journal of Polynesian Society,* vol. 28, 1919, p. 219.

3 Madgwick, *Aotea*, p. 99. W. Wilson, 'Nomenclature, legends etc as supplied by the Maori in South Westland, 1897'*,* p. 111, Anderson Papers, MS-Papers-0148-112, Alexander Turnbull Library. Wilson's South Westland informants explained that a tohunga was a very clever man.

4 Madgwick, *Aotea*, p. 99.

5 *Nelson Examiner*, 16 September 1857.

6 Charles Ollivier, 'The Expedition to the West Coast', *Press*, 8 November 1862, p. 2.

7 *Grey River Argus*, 23 August 1866. Madgwick, *Aotea*, pp.102-104. Rochford, *Myth*, p. 3.

8 John Pascoe, *The Haast is in South Westland*, A.H. & A.W. Reed, 1966, p. 26 (note). Philip Ross May, *The West Coast Gold Rushes*, Pegasus Press, 1962, p. 30 (note). A. Charles and Neil C. Begg, *The World of John Boultbee: Including an account of sealing in Australia and New Zealand*, Whitcoulls, 1979, p. 140 (note).

9 Ollivier, 'The Expedition ...'*,* op. cit., p. 2.

10 Ibid.

11 *Press*, 8 November 1862.

12 Ibid.

13 Anon, 'Notes of the voyage of the Cutter *Nugget*', *Invercargill Times*, 20 November 1863, p. 2.

14 *Otago Witness*, 17 January 1922.

15 Robert Preston Bain, 'Journal of an Expedition to the West Coast of the Province of Canterbury, N.Z. undertaken for the purpose of Surveying part of the Coast of that Province, 1863-64'. Typed transcript, Nelson Provincial Museum. Robert Preston Bain to Canterbury Provincial Government Secretary, 1864, Canterbury Provincial Government Records, Archives New Zealand (Christchurch Office), ICPS 287 1243/1864.

16 Bain, 'Journal', op. cit.

17 *West Coast Times*, 10 April 1866.

18 *West Coast Times*, 13 February 1867

19 *West Coast Times*, 10 December 1867, p. 2.

20 *West Coast Times*, 25 September 1873.

21 *West Coast Times*, 9 October 1873.

22 *Arrow Observer*, 19 December 1873, p. 3.

Chapter 2

1   *West Coast Times*, 28 November 1874.
2   *Appendix to the Journals of the House of Representatives* (AJHR), 1875, D-5, p. 16. *AJHR*, 1879, H-9a, p. 73-74.
3   *AJHR*, 1875, D-5, p. 16.
4   *AJHR*, 1875, D-5, p. 18. *Lake Wakatip* Mail, 9 March 1876. *West Coast Times*, 12 September 1876, p. 2.
5   *West Coast Times*, 9 February 1876, p. 2.
6   *AJHR*, 1879, H-9, pp. 12-13. *AJHR*, 1879, H-9a, p. 45, p. 50.
7   *AJHR*, 1877, H-28, p. 3. *AJHR*, 1879, H-9a, p. 98.
8   *AJHR*, 1879, H-9, p. 16. *AJHR*, 1879, H-9a, p. 8.
9   *AJHR*, 1879, H-9a, p. 105.
10 *AJHR*, 1875, D-5, p. 9. *AJHR*, 1879, H-9a, pp. 60-63.
11 *AJHR*, 1884, Volume 1, session 2, C-1, appendix 5, p. 76.
12 *Kumara Times*, 16 December 1887.

Chapter 3

1   Frank Heveldt, taped interview, 1961, T210, Sound Archives/Nga Taonga Korero.
2   *AJHR*, 1877, H-28, p. 10. *AJHR*, 1879, H-9a, p. 74. Death certificate for Rosalie Witski, Registrar of Births, Deaths and Marriages.
3   John Heveldt, taped interview, 1961, T238, Sound Archives/Nga Taonga Korero.
4   *Kumara Times*, 19 May 1888.

List of Sources

Chapter 1

Anon. 'Notes of the voyage of the cutter *Nugget'*. *Invercargill Times*, 20 November 1863, p. 2.

Anon. 'Supposed Loss of the Whaling Barque *Pacific*'. *Nelson Examiner*, 16 September 1857.

Bain, Robert Preston. 'Journal of an Expedition to the West Coast of the Province of Canterbury, N.Z. undertaken for the purpose of Surveying part of the Coast of that Province, 1863-64', 28 September 1863–25 February 1864. Nelson Provincial Museum.

Beattie, Herries. 'Traditions and Legends collected from the natives of Murihiku'. *Journal of the Polynesian Society*, Vol. 28, 1919, p. 219.

Begg, A. Charles and Neil C. *The World of John Boultbee: Including an account of sealing in Australia and New Zealand.* Whitcoulls Publishers, 1979.

Grey River Argus, 23 August 1866.

Hooker, R.H. *The Archaeology of the South Westland Maori.* New Zealand Forest Service, Hokitika, 1986.

Ingram, C.W.N. *New Zealand Shipwrecks 1795–1970.* A.H. & A.W. Reed, 4th edition, 1972.

Madgwick, Paul. *Aotea: A History of the South Westland Maori.* Printed by Greymouth Evening Star, 1992.

May, Philip Ross. *The West Coast Gold Rushes.* Pegasus Press, 1962.

Ollivier, Charles. *The Expedition to the West Coast. Press*, 8 November 1862 p. 5.

Pascoe, John. *The Haast is in South Westland.* A.H. & A.W. Reed, 1966.

Roxburgh, Irvine. *Jackson Bay: A Centennial History.* A.H & A.W. Reed, 1976.

West Coast Times, 10 April 1866.

West Coast Times, 5-14 February 1867.

Wilson, W. 'Nomenclature, legends etc as supplied by the Maori in South Westland, 1897'. MS-Papers-0148-112, Alexander Turnbull Library.

Chapter 2

Appendices to the Journal of the House of Representatives. 1875, D-5. 1877, H-28. 1879, H-9 & H-9a. 1884, Volume 1, Session 2, C-1, Appendix 5.

Pascoe, John. *The Haast is in South Westland.* A.H. & A.W. Reed, 1966.

Roxburgh, Irvine. *Jackson Bay: A Centennial History.* A.H & A.W. Reed, 1976.

West Coast Times, 28 November, 1874 p. 2.

Chapter 3

Appendices to the Journal of the House of Representatives. 1877, H-28, p. 10.
Personal communication with Heveldt Family historian, Francis Henry Heveldt.
Sound Archives recordings, reference numbers T210 (Frank Heveldt) and T238 (John
  Heveldt).

Chapters 4-12

Oral history interviews with the following:

Buchanan, Henry John. Interviewed 16, 17 December 1995 and 27, 28 January 1996.
Cowan, Bernard Homersham. Interviewed 25 April 1996.
Cowan, Myra Edith née Roberts. Interviewed 25 April 1996.
Cron, Allan Andrew. Interviewed 14, 15 June 1996.
Eggeling, Milcah Elizabeth (Betty) née Buchanan. Interviewed 15, 16 November 1997.
Hill, Ruth Ida (Ruby) née Eggeling. Interviewed 15 February 1998.
Jones, Mary. Interviewed 18, 19 February 1997.
Mackey, Ann Patricia née Nolan. Interviewed 15 June 1996.
Nolan, Desmond Joseph. Interviewed 17 and 31 March 1996.

Tapes and abstracts are located at the Oral History Centre, Alexander Turnbull
  Library, Wellington, and at the West Coast Historical Museum, Hokitika.

Index